This Day in Florida History

UNIVERSITY PRESS OF FLORIDA

Florida A&M University, Tallahassee
Florida Atlantic University, Boca Raton
Florida Gulf Coast University, Ft. Myers
Florida International University, Miami
Florida State University, Tallahassee
New College of Florida, Sarasota
University of Central Florida, Orlando
University of Florida, Gainesville
University of North Florida, Jacksonville
University of South Florida, Tampa
University of West Florida, Pensacola

This Day in Florida History

Andrew K. Frank,
J. Hendry Miller,
and Tarah Luke

University Press of Florida
Gainesville · Tallahassee
Tampa · Boca Raton
Pensacola · Orlando
Miami · Jacksonville
Ft. Myers · Sarasota

25 24 23 22 21 20   6 5 4 3 2 1

Library of Congress Control Number: 2019955094
ISBN 978-0-8130-6822-0

The University Press of Florida is the scholarly publishing agency for the State
University System of Florida, comprising Florida A&M University, Florida Atlantic
University, Florida Gulf Coast University, Florida International University, Florida
State University, New College of Florida, University of Central Florida, University
of Florida, University of North Florida, University of South Florida, and University
of West Florida.

University Press of Florida
2046 NE Waldo Road
Suite 2100
Gainesville, FL 32609
http://upress.ufl.edu

PREFACE

The seventy-fifth anniversary of the University Press of Florida of-
fers an opportunity to reflect on the events, people, and themes that
best illuminate the history of Florida. Much has changed over the past
seventy-five years, both in terms of the development of the state and
in the maturation of the history profession. Florida's population today is roughly ten times larger than it was in 1945. The population
has moved southward, transforming the small towns of Orlando and
Miami into cosmopolitan cities, and the state has become a destination for immigrants and tourists from across the globe. The history
profession also has changed as scholars have expanded the range of
historical inquiry to include people and topics that were once deemed
inconsequential. It is in this spirit that we offer *This Day in Florida History* and its 366 entries.

In 1945, when UPF opened, the events for this type of volume would
have been simple to choose. It would have been filled with elections,
important legislation, city incorporations, inventions, and famous
politicians. It would have emphasized the perspectives of the wealthy,
of white communities, and of men. The entries would have been a
celebration of achievements and progress without much awareness of
the costs of development and change. In 1945, few paid much attention to the presence of the Spanish in the colonial era or of enslaved
Africans in the Old South. Residents from Cuba and the Caribbean
who called Florida home for centuries were deemed unimportant, and
Native Americans were dismissed as savages who were inevitably on
their way toward extinction. The volume would have had a different
geographic feel as well; the entries would have largely focused on the

Panhandle, as the population shift in the state that followed World War II had not yet occurred.

This Day in Florida History reflects these changes in Florida and in historical sensibilities more generally. Rather than representing the 366 most important and best-known events in Florida history, the entries that follow illuminate the state's diversity and the various themes that explain it. The topics of some entries would fit comfortably in the imagined volume from 1945, even if the interpretations of them may not. Most of the topics, though, would not have been included in such a volume. Some entries may be familiar to readers; others may not. Entries cover civil rights protests, revolts by Apalachee Indians, crashes at the Daytona 500, and disputes over the drainage of the Everglades. They include the capture of the Seminole warrior Osceola, the establishment of Walt Disney World and of Fort Mosé, and the recurrence of hurricanes. The 366 entries hardly encompass the entirety of Florida history, of course, and we hope that this volume sparks interest in learning more. To this end, we have listed a suggested reading for each entry in the volume.

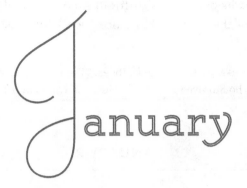

January

JANUARY 1

On January 1, 1923, a bruised Frances "Fannie" Taylor falsely claimed that an unnamed African American man assaulted and raped her. She made up the explosive charges to explain the bruises from her abusive lover and otherwise cover up her infidelity. A posse of white men formed in the town of Sumner to protect white supremacy and the sanctity of white womanhood, and it attacked and threatened the

residents of the neighboring all-black town of Rosewood. Two of the white assailants were killed when they stormed a house where community members had fled for safety. The ensuing six days of violence led to the deaths of at least six African Americans and the evacuation and razing of the town. It has since been known as the Rosewood massacre.

FOR FURTHER READING: Maxine D. Jones, "The Rosewood Massacre and the Women Who Survived It," *Florida Historical Quarterly* 76, no. 2 (1997): 193–208.

JANUARY 2

On January 2, 1936, Dick and Julia Pope opened the roadside attraction Cypress Gardens in Winter Haven. Its financial scale dwarfed that of earlier attractions, and it initiated a new phase in the history of Florida theme parks. It began largely as a botanical garden and quickly expanded to include an array of waterskiing shows that earned its nickname as "Water Ski Capital of the World." The site became a popular location to film movies and commercials but struggled to compete in the post-Disney world. In 2010 Legoland purchased the site, which had been closed for several years, and integrated some of the botanical gardens into a new theme park on the site.

FOR FURTHER READING: Lou Vickers, *Cypress Gardens: America's Tropical Wonderland: How Dick Pope Invented Florida* (Gainesville: University Press of Florida, 2010).

JANUARY 3

On January 3, 1987, Wayne Mixon began the shortest term as Florida's governor. Mixon served only three days, replacing Governor Daniel Robert "Bob" Graham, who resigned to begin his term as a US senator. Mixon, who had served two terms as lieutenant governor under Graham, took on the position as a temporary measure to fill a gap created by the inaugural calendar. Mixon left office on January 6 when newly elected Robert "Bob" Martinez took the oath of office. Mixon's position as governor would be his last public office.

FOR FURTHER READING: Allen Morris and Joan Perry Morris, eds., *The Florida Handbook, 2011–2012,* 33rd biennial edition (Tallahassee: Peninsular, 2011).

JANUARY 4

On January 4, 2000, Florida State University won its second national title in football. Led by standout wide receiver Peter Warrick, the Seminoles defeated Virginia Tech 46–29 in a thrilling Sugar Bowl game. They overcame Virginia Tech and its quarterback, Michael Vick. The game epitomized two decades of dominance by teams from Florida. Along with the University of Florida and the University of Miami, FSU changed the landscape of college football in the 1980s and 1990s. From 1983 to 2001, the three teams combined to win eight national championships and consistently finished in the top 5 of the year-end rankings.

FOR FURTHER READING: Bob Boyles and Paul Guido, *The USA Today College Football Encyclopedia, 2009–2010: A Comprehensive Modern Reference to America's Most Colorful Sport, 1953-Present* (New York: Skyhorse, 2009).

JANUARY 5

On January 5, 1942, British Prime Minister Winston Churchill flew to South Florida for a brief break from international diplomacy. Churchill stayed for five days in Pompano Beach at the house of US Secretary

of State Edward Stettinius. Churchill flew to the United States shortly after the attack on Pearl Harbor to coordinate the war efforts of the two countries. The meetings of high-ranking officials in Washington, DC, known as the Arcadia Conference, lasted from December 22 to January 12. The prime minister spent most of the time as President Franklin Delano Roosevelt's guest. The excursion to Florida provided a brief respite from the arduous planning at the conference, and Churchill hoped the Florida trip would prevent him from overstaying his welcome.

FOR FURTHER READING: Celia Sandys, *Chasing Churchill: The Travels of Winston Churchill* (London: Unicorn, 2014).

JANUARY 6

On January 6, 1836, a group of Seminole Indians attacked William Cooley's plantation and killed Cooley's wife, their children, and a tutor. The plantation was on the New River in what is now Fort Lauderdale. The attack was retribution for what the Natives perceived as Cooley's betrayal of his role as justice of the peace the year before. In late 1835, white settlers killed Chief Alabama. Cooley discovered the perpetrators, only to have a county court dismiss the charges on account of "insufficient evidence." Word of the so-called New River massacre or Cooley massacre helped white Americans justify the ensuing Second Seminole War.

FOR FURTHER READING: Andrew K. Frank, *Before the Pioneers: Indians, Settlers, Slaves, and the Founding of Miami* (Gainesville: University Press of Florida, 2017).

JANUARY 7

On January 7, 1861, local militia from Fernandina captured Fort Marion in the name of the newly formed Confederacy. The capture of Fort Marion occurred a few days before Florida formally voted to secede from the United States, but the US military had already abandoned the fort that it deemed unworthy of defending. Only Ordnance Sergeant Henry Douglas stayed behind as caretaker. When the Florida militiamen arrived, Douglas would only cede control of the fort after the militia signed a receipt accepting responsibility for the historic fort. The militia then took most of the artillery and other supplies back to Fernandina. The Confederacy controlled Fort Marion until March 12, 1862.

FOR FURTHER READING: Daniel L. Schafer, *Thunder on the River: The Civil War in Northeast Florida* (Gainesville: University Press of Florida, 2010).

JANUARY 8

On January 8, 1842, the St. Augustine *News* published "Notes on the Passage across the Everglades." Written to relay details about a Second Seminole War engagement, "Notes" provided one of the first highly detailed published accounts of the Everglades. It revealed many of the ecological challenges the soldiers confronted, including the region's "boundless expanse of saw-grass and water, occasionally interspersed with little islands, all of which are overflowed." The account described for the public the exotic flora and fauna of the interior as well as the presence of islands and mangroves in the wetlands. In many ways it shaped the public's fascination with the region as both a uniquely exotic environment and a potentially untapped source of economic opportunity.

FOR FURTHER READING: Michael Grumwald, *The Swamp: The Everglades, Florida, and the Politics of Paradise* (New York: Simon and Schuster, 2006).

JANUARY 9

On January 9, 1824, Alexander Scott, the tax collector in Pensacola, pleaded with Congress to not appoint someone to help regulate trade in the town. The United States had recently claimed Florida from Spain and scrambled to fill administrative roles throughout the territory. Scott insisted that appointing another administrator was a needless expense, especially in what he deemed the sleepy town of Pensacola. He declared that he was more than capable of taking on the meager obligations that would arise from the local economy. The town had only a few hundred white and black inhabitants, and the local economy was based on trading for deerskins with local Creek Indians, a trade that federally appointed Indian agents would handle. The rest, Scott explained, was hardly worth regulating at all because "no teas wines &cc are, or probably ever will be imported into that place."

FOR FURTHER READING: John James Clune and Margo S. Stringfield, *Historic Pensacola* (Gainesville: University Press of Florida, 2009).

JANUARY 10

On January 10, 1861, Florida became the third state to secede from the United States. The delegates to the secession convention were overwhelmingly slaveholders who justified their actions on account of the abolitionist policies of Lincoln and the Republican Party. They declared that they had no choice but to separate from a federal government whose leaders "proclaimed hostility to our institutions." The final vote tally was 62–7, but 65 men ultimately signed Florida's secession ordinance. Of all of the Confederate states, Florida was by far the least populated and was widely seen as still being the frontier. This perception led contemporaries to ridicule it as the "smallest tadpole in the dirty pool of secession."

FOR FURTHER READING: Tracy J. Revels, *Florida's Civil War: Terrible Sacrifices* (Macon, GA: Mercer University Press, 2016).

JANUARY 11

On January 11, 1943, a writ of habeas corpus was issued in the case of Emmanuel Pollock, an African American laborer from Brevard County. His experience revealed the plight of African Americans under Jim Crow, and his legal case set the stage for many challenges to the status quo. Pollock's path to the court system resulted from a common experience. Like many African Americans in the South, he took out a $5 advance from his employer only to leave his job after several months for a better one. Authorities arrested Pollock for failing to repay his employer and charged him with an intent to defraud. Without the aid of legal counsel, Pollock was convicted under a 1919 law and sentenced to pay a $100 fine or spend sixty days in jail. The Florida Supreme Court ultimately upheld the conviction. The following year, on April 10, the US Supreme Court overturned the ruling, determining that the Florida law violated the Thirteenth Amendment and the Peonage Act of 1867.

FOR FURTHER READING: Michael J. Klarman, *From Jim Crow to Civil Rights: The Supreme Court and the Struggle for Racial Equality* (New York: Oxford University Press, 2004).

Men in a Florida chain gang collecting scrape for turpentine, ca. 1910.

JANUARY 12

On January 12, 1838, Governor William Duval declared the interior of the Florida Panhandle to be "the most desirable and valuable region in all the Southern Country." Having just traveled from St. Augustine to Pensacola, Duval foresaw the rapid development of the region known as Middle Florida. In a letter to US Secretary of War John C. Calhoun, Duval justified the forced removal of the Seminoles as part of a larger plan to protect and extend slavery into the territory's agricultural fields and expand established cattle herds. Duval's vision for Middle Florida quickly came to reality, as it became the heart of Florida's cotton belt and its population of enslaved African Americans.

FOR FURTHER READING: Edward Baptist, *Creating an Old South: Middle Florida's Plantation Frontier before the Civil War* (Chapel Hill: University of North Carolina Press, 2002).

JANUARY 13

On January 13, 1871, John Crawford, a member of the Florida legislature from Wakulla County, was arrested under the federal Enforcement Act. This law sought to protect the rights of African Americans who increasingly faced widespread voter intimidation and suppression by local white authorities. Provisos in the Enforcement Act would later be incorporated into the Voting Rights Act of 1965. Many prominent Floridians were indicted and found guilty under the Enforcement Act for various acts of intimidation and voter fraud. In this case, though, the act revealed the power of Jim Crow. Despite evidence of wrongdoing, the court dismissed Crawford's case because the original act granted immunity to sitting elected officials.

FOR FURTHER READING: Joe Richardson, *African Americans in the Reconstruction of Florida, 1865–1877* (Tuscaloosa: University of Alabama Press, 2008).

On January 14, 1919, Mary Catherine Lawhon Kahn was born in Arran, Florida. She was one of 84,000 women who served in the US Navy as part of the Women Accepted for Volunteer Emergency Service (WAVES) during World War II. Kahn enlisted in October 1943 and served in Key West during the war as a "2nd class mailman." Prohibited from combat assignments, WAVES enlistees took on responsibilities previously fulfilled by men to make more men available to serve overseas. The women performed many functions, from training soldiers to use anti-aircraft guns to serving as clerks. When the war ended the unit was dissolved.

FOR FURTHER READING: Evan Bachner, *Making WAVES: Navy Women of World War II* (New York: Abrams, 2008).

Mary Catherine Lawhon Kahn during World War II.

JANUARY 15

On January 15, 1790, Spanish Governor Vincent Manual Zéspedes decreed that free African Americans in Florida could not own land. The new policy overturned more than a century of practice in the Spanish colony, as it evicted African American families from their farms unless the family lived with a white man. Although Spanish colonists enslaved Africans in Florida as elsewhere in the Americas, Florida consistently offered freedom to African Americans who escaped slavery in English colonies or the United States. The newcomers became subjects of the Spanish Crown, even if their freedoms were restricted in the colony.

FOR FURTHER READING: Jane Landers, *Black Society in Spanish Florida* (Urbana: University of Illinois Press, 1999).

JANUARY 16

On January 16, 1897, Henry Flagler opened his Royal Palm Hotel in the newly incorporated city of Miami. The establishment of the hotel transformed South Florida's small community into a bustling tourist destination. Located on Biscayne Bay on the north bank of the Miami River, the hotel was built on top of 2,000 years of continuous occupations by Tequesta and Seminole Indians, Spanish missionaries, enslaved African Americans, US soldiers, and others. The hotel featured five stories, elevators, and a swimming pool, and it attracted guests

from across the globe. The glamorous hotel was destroyed by the hurricane of 1926.

FOR FURTHER READING: Andrew K. Frank, *Before the Pioneers: Indians, Settlers, Slaves, and the Founding of Miami* (Gainesville: University Press of Florida, 2017).

JANUARY 17

On January 17, 1991, charges were brought against sex worker Aileen Wuornos in Volusia County for the murder of seven men in northern and Central Florida. Wuornos, who shot each man at close range, proclaimed that she needed to do so to fend off rapists. Rather than acts of self-defense, the pattern of violence pointed to Wuornos being a serial killer. She was convicted of six murders and sentenced to death. Wuornos was executed on October 9, 2002, by lethal injection. The 2003 movie *Monster* brought national attention to the story. Charlize Theron won a Best Actress Oscar for her portrayal of Wuornos.

FOR FURTHER READING: Joseph Michael Reynolds, *Dead Ends: The Pursuit, Conviction, and Execution of Serial Killer Aileen Wuornos* (New York: Open Road, 2016).

JANUARY 18

On January 18, 1849, the village of Tampa was officially incorporated around the US military outpost of Fort Brooke. The United States built the fort in 1824 along the Hillsborough River to enforce the 1823 Treaty of Moultrie Creek. This treaty confined the Seminoles to the southern interior of the Florida Peninsula. The US military used the fort as a base to conduct raids into Indian country to kill, capture, harass, and otherwise force Seminoles to give up their lands. In 1980, developers discovered a Second Seminole War–era cemetery in the area. After a negotiation between Tampa and Seminole tribal leaders, the Seminole Tribe of Florida obtained a reservation in Tampa to relocate their ancestors' remains and conduct economic development. Today, the Hard Rock Tampa sits on that site.

TAMPA BAY ON THE GULF OF MEXICO.

FOR FURTHER READING: Canter Brown, *Tampa before the Civil War* (Tampa: University of Tampa Press, 1999).

JANUARY 19

On January 19, 1971, President Richard Nixon halted construction of the Cross Florida Barge Canal with an executive order. The proposed canal was designed to cut across the Florida Peninsula and connect the Gulf of Mexico with the Atlantic Ocean. Hopes of such an aquatic connection—whether natural or constructed—had preoccupied Florida's colonizers for 300 years; they argued that a shortcut through Florida would be useful for naval defense as well as a lucrative shipping route. Environmentalists, spearheaded by Marjorie Carr, worked tirelessly to convince the public and politicians of the devastating environmental and economic consequences, and they succeeded in halting construction.

FOR FURTHER READING: Steven Noll and David Tegeder, *Ditch of Dreams: The Cross Florida Barge Canal and the Struggle for Florida's Future* (Gainesville: University Press of Florida, 2009).

JANUARY 20

On January 20, 1834, the Florida Territorial Legislative Council dissolved Fayette County, which was created out of Jackson County in 1832. Fayette County was created when Webbville business owners and real estate speculators pushed to make their town the county seat rather than Marianna. Using their influence in the council, they temporarily succeeded in splitting Jackson County into two. The following year, residents of both Panhandle counties, displeased with the land schemes and a naked power grab, formally petitioned to have the two counties reunited.

FOR FURTHER READING: Jerrell H. Shofner, *Jackson County, Florida: A History* (Marianna, FL: Jackson County Historical Association, 1985).

JANUARY 21

On January 21, 1802, Native men from the Mikasuki town in present-day Leon County attacked Jose Bonnelli's plantation in Matanzas near St. Augustine. The men killed Bonnelli's oldest son, took his wife and five other children captive, and burned the property. Captive-taking raids occurred regularly in early Florida and early America more generally. Native Americans and Europeans raided towns and villages, stole horses and cattle, and harassed travelers when they ventured out of their communities. Captive taking had roots in the ancient Southeast. Centuries before the arrival of the Spanish, southeastern Indians incorporated captives of war into their communities to replace deceased kin. The capture of the Bonnelli family followed this tradition.

FOR FURTHER READING: Christina Snyder, *Slavery in Indian Country: The Changing Face of Captivity in Early America* (Cambridge, MA: Harvard University Press, 2010).

January 22

On January 22, 1912, Henry Flagler rode on the first passenger train from South Florida to Key West. The journey was the first on a newly constructed leg of the Florida East Coast Railway, an extension Flagler hoped would transform the American economy. Flagler was motivated to extend the railroad to Key West because of the financial opportunities of the opening of the Panama Canal. The railroad connected the southern tip of the Florida Peninsula with Key West 128 miles away. Critics of this risky decision called it Flagler's Folly. The railway was destroyed by the 1935 Labor Day Hurricane and was later replaced with the Overseas Highway.

FOR FURTHER READING: Les Standiford, *Last Train to Paradise: Henry Flagler and the Spectacular Rise and Fall of a Railroad That Crossed an Ocean* (New York: Three Rivers, 2002).

January 23

On January 23, 2013, Florida announced that it would open Silver Springs as a public facility. The artesian springs at the site originally opened as a tourist attraction for predominantly white northerners shortly after the Civil War. Excluded from the park until it was desegregated in 1969, African Americans visited neighboring and less scenic Paradise Park one mile away. One of the most popular and enduring forms of entertainment at Silver Springs was Ross Allen's Reptile Institute, which he ran for forty-six years; he conducted research and entertained tourists with alligators, crocodiles, and snakes and was bitten so often by rattlesnakes that his body produced its own antivenom. In 1993, the state purchased the struggling park and allowed its owners to lease and temporarily keep it open. In 2013, the state took over and merged the park with protected public lands that surrounded it. Today Silver Springs State Park consists of roughly 5,000 acres along the Silver River. No signs remain of Paradise Park, which closed when Silver Springs was desegregated, as it has been allowed to be covered by underbrush.

FOR FURTHER READING: Lu Vickers and Cynthia Wilson-Graham, *Remembering Paradise Park: Tourism and Segregation at Silver Springs* (Gainesville: University Press of Florida, 2015).

JANUARY 24

On January 24, 1704, Colonel James Moore, a former governor of South Carolina, led a raiding force of 1,500 Creek Indians and fifty Englishmen against the Spanish mission Nuestra Señora de la Concepcíon de Ayubale. The slave raid helped destroy the extensive system of missions that the Spanish erected in Apalachee country in the middle of the Florida Panhandle. A generation earlier, the region had eleven mission towns, each with its own friar, and a missionized population of roughly 8,000 to 9,000. Slave raids like Moore's resulted in the capture and sale of tens of thousands of Indians from the American South. Some Native slaves remained in southern colonies, but most were exported to the Caribbean.

FOR FURTHER READING: Alejandra Dubcovsky, "'All of Us Will Have to Pay for These Activities': Colonial and Native Narratives of the 1704 Attack on Ayubale," *Native South* 10 (2017): 1–18.

JANUARY 25

On January 25, 1947, Alphonse "Al" Capone died at his Palm Island estate in Miami Beach. Better known as Scarface, Capone emerged as one of the most notorious criminals of the twentieth century. He amassed tremendous wealth through racketeering and liquor trafficking during Prohibition and for seven years led the Chicago Outfit organized crime syndicate. Capone purchased his Florida mansion in 1928 for $40,000 in

Al Capone in Miami Beach.

cash. Attracted by South Florida's lifestyle, Capone tried to repair his public image in Miami, but he remained infamous for his role as a mob boss and alleged complicity in the St. Valentine's Day Massacre. Federal authorities never convicted Capone for his mob activities and instead convicted him of tax evasion.

FOR FURTHER READING: Stephen C. Bousquet, "The Gangster in Our Midst: Al Capone in South Florida, 1930–1947," *Florida Historical Quarterly* 76, no. 3 (1998): 297–309.

JANUARY 26

On January 26, 1957, Florida State University expelled John Boardman for organizing a racially integrated event at the segregated university. Shortly after the US Supreme Court ruled that public facilities could not be segregated, Boardman, a white PhD student, invited three international students from neighboring Florida A&M University to an FSU-sponsored Christmas party. FSU President Doak Campbell declared that the expulsion demonstrated the university administration's broad authority and would further limit the involvement of FSU students in the growing civil rights movement. Boardman eventually finished his doctorate at Syracuse University. FSU's football stadium is named for Campbell.

FOR FURTHER READING: Glenda Alice Rabby, *The Pain and the Promise: The Struggle for Civil Rights in Tallahassee* (Athens: University of Georgia Press, 1999).

Left to right: Civil rights activists Reverend C. K. Steele, John Boardman, and Reverend J. Raymond Henderson.

JANUARY 27

On January 27, 1967, the *Apollo 1* capsule caught fire during a launch rehearsal at Cape Kennedy, the NASA hub and launch site previously known as Cape Canaveral. American astronauts Gus Grissom, Edward White, and Roger Chaffee died in the fire. The launch would have been the first low-orbital test of the lunar landing mission. A NASA investigation did not pinpoint the source of the electrical fire but rather pointed to several factors that exacerbated the disaster. These issues included the use of highly combustible nylon in the cabin's pressurized pure oxygen environment. NASA retired *Apollo 1* in the aftermath of the disaster.

FOR FURTHER READING: Colin Burgess, Kate Doolan, and Bert Vis, *Fallen Astronauts: Heroes Who Died Reaching for the Moon*, revised edition (Lincoln: University of Nebraska Press, 2016).

JANUARY 28

On January 28, 1986, the space shuttle *Challenger* exploded seven seconds after taking off from Cape Canaveral. The accident killed seven astronauts: Francis R. "Dick" Scobee, Michael J. Smith, Ronald McNair, Ellison Onizuka, Judith Resnik, Gregory Jarvis, and Christa McAuliffe. The event was televised live nationally, and the inclusion of schoolteacher McAuliffe ensured that students across the country watched it. NASA went on a thirty-two-month launch hiatus after the disaster, refraining from any flights into space. Coincidentally, all of NASA's human fatalities occurred within six consecutive calendar days. The *Apollo 1* fire occurred on January 27, 1967, the *Challenger* explosion on the 28th, and the *Columbia* disaster on February 1, 2003. As a result, NASA observes the last week in January as Astronaut Remembrance Week.

FOR FURTHER READING: Colin Burgess, Kate Doolan, and Bert Vis, *Fallen Astronauts: Heroes Who Died Reaching for the Moon*, revised edition (Lincoln: University of Nebraska Press, 2016).

On January 29, 1877, the US Congress established an advisory commission to determine how to handle the contested electoral votes from Florida and three other southern states. During the presidential election of 1876, white vigilante groups across the South attempted to restrict African Americans from voting and otherwise tried to redeem the region from what they called "Republican" or "Negro rule." The commission ultimately gave all of the contested electoral votes—including Florida's four—to Republican Rutherford B. Hayes. Shortly after the commission made its ruling, federal forces withdrew from the South and ultimately allowed white Democrats to strip away many of the freedoms African Americans enjoyed during Reconstruction. The so-called Compromise of 1877 ushered in the era of Jim Crow.

FOR FURTHER READING: Michael F. Holt, *By One Vote: The Disputed Presidential Election of 1876* (Lawrence: University of Kansas Press, 2008).

JANUARY 30

On January 30, 1838, Seminole military leader Osceola died in prison at Fort Moultrie in Charleston, South Carolina. The US military captured Osceola when he and a group of warriors and diplomats attended a prearranged meeting to discuss a truce with the United States during the Second Seminole War. US military officers hoped the capture of Osceola and the warriors with him would end the war. This belief led the officers to defy orders and military practice by ignoring the Seminoles' white flag of diplomacy. After the other warriors escaped from prison in St. Augustine, the military moved Osceola to Charleston, where he became a cause célèbre. After his death, Osceola became a symbol of the anti–Seminole War movement in the United States.

FOR FURTHER READING: John K. Mahon, *History of the Second Seminole War, 1835–1842* (Gainesville: University Press of Florida, 1967).

JANUARY 31

On January 31, 1963, the Florida Supreme Court approved a district reapportionment plan put forth as a statute by the Florida legislature. By the early 1960s, Florida's population had shifted from the Panhandle and rural areas and became overwhelmingly urban and suburban. This transformation, largely the result of the growth of Central and South Florida cities, distorted the system of representation designed for its earlier rural character. A group of rural legislators known as the Pork Chop Gang controlled state politics, leaving the interests of most voters unrepresented. In 1962 the Pork Chop Gang offered their own resolution that voters rejected because it made only modest changes in representation. The final reapportionment plan brought more adequate representation to Florida and helped modernize the Sunshine State.

FOR FURTHER READING: Mary E. Adkins, *Making Modern Florida: How the Spirit of Reform Shaped a New State Constitution* (Gainesville: University Press of Florida, 2016).

February

FEBRUARY 1

On February 1, 1929, Bok Tower Gardens opened to the public in Lake Wales. Hundreds of guests, including President Calvin Coolidge, attended the official dedication of the 250-acre bird sanctuary. Edward Bok, the editor of *Ladies Home Journal*, hoped that the area would attract birds from around the region and introduced various species to help start the park. Although his attempt to introduce non-native flamingos failed, the general bird population thrived. They made their homes in and near the thousands of planted trees and bushes—live oaks, azaleas, gardenias, magnolias, sabal palms, and others.

FOR FURTHER READING: Tim Hollis, *Dixie before Disney: 100 Years of Roadside Fun* (Jackson: University of Mississippi Press, 1999).

FEBRUARY 2

On February 2, 1980, the FBI sting operation Abscam became public knowledge. Short for "Abdul Scam," the public corruption investigation ultimately resulted in the arrest and conviction of Florida Congressman Richard Kelly, six other US congressmen, and several local politicians from New Jersey and Pennsylvania. In the operation, a fictitious Middle Eastern businessman attempted to bribe politicians in exchange for political favors. Kelly, a Republican from Zephyrhills, was filmed taking a $25,000 bribe and stuffing it and some cigars into his pockets; he spent the money before being arrested. Kelly proclaimed his innocence and insisted that he was running his own sting operation against corrupt federal agents. He ultimately served thirteen months in prison.

FOR FURTHER READING: Craig Pittman, *Oh, Florida! How America's Weirdest State Influences the Rest of the Country* (New York: St. Martin's Press, 2016).

FEBRUARY 3

On February 3, 1885, Susan B. Anthony wrote to Floridian Julia Seiver to inquire about her helping to rally support for the women's suffrage movement in Florida. The movement had been struggling to gain traction in Florida even among white reformers. Instead of pushing for the vote, many white women emphasized temperance and maintaining racial segregation. Seiver thought differently and told Anthony that she wished she was healthy enough to go on a speaking tour for the "noble cause" because "the indifference manifested by the [white] women of the South is truly deplorable." Despite Seiver and Anthony's efforts, Florida women did not get the right to vote until 1920.

FOR FURTHER READING: Doris Weatherford, *They Dared to Dream: Florida Women Who Shaped History* (Gainesville: University Press of Florida, 2015).

FEBRUARY 4

On February 4, 1865, Dr. Esther Hill Hawks lamented in her diary the poor condition and character of Florida's poor white "crackers." Hawks, who was born in New Hampshire, moved to Florida just before the Civil War. When war broke out she applied to serve as a Union nurse. Despite graduating from the New England Medical College, she was denied a medical position. Instead she worked as a teacher, often assisting her doctor husband in Florida and South Carolina. Near the end of the war, she fled Charleston and returned to Florida, where she primarily used her teaching and medical skills in the African American community. Hawks made little headway with whites, who resisted her for both her political views and her gender. Hawks left Florida in 1870 and moved to Lynn, Massachusetts, where she continued to practice medicine.

FOR FURTHER READING: Gerald Schwartz, ed., *A Woman Doctor's Civil War: Esther Hill Hawks' Diary* (Columbia: University of South Carolina Press, 1984).

A Cracker Cowboy, by Frederic Remington, 1895.

FEBRUARY 5

On February 5, 1988, Panamanian dictator Manuel Noriega was indicted by a federal jury in Miami for crimes related to drug trafficking, money laundering, and racketeering. Noriega was a longtime US ally. American officials overlooked his connections to drug smuggling in order to earn diplomatic favor against communists in Latin America. The fall of the Soviet Union and the shift in focus in the federal government's war on drugs ultimately made Noriega an expendable ally. American forces invaded Panama in 1989 and captured Noriega in January 1990. A federal court in Miami convicted Noriega on several charges and sentenced him to forty years in prison.

FOR FURTHER READING: Russell Crandall, *Gunboat Democracy: US Interventions in the Dominican Republic, Grenada, and Panama* (Lanham, MD: Rowman and Littlefield, 2006).

FEBRUARY 6

On February 6, 1895, the last of three significant freezes in the winter of 1894–1895 struck Florida. The freezes had terrible effects on Florida's citrus industry. Citrus production dropped to almost zero, compared to six million boxes the previous year, and would not reach pre-freeze levels until 1909. Florida's emerging tourist industry also suffered in the freezes. As part of a transcontinental rivalry, California farmers, land speculators, and hoteliers poked fun at Florida, noting that Florida vacationers needed heat in their rooms and Florida citrus was at too much risk from cold weather to be a safe investment. The freezes pushed the citrus industry farther south in the state and helped city boosters promote newly formed towns along the southern Gulf and Atlantic shores.

FOR FURTHER READING: Henry Knight, *Tropic of Hopes: California, Florida, and the Selling of American Paradise, 1869–1929* (Gainesville: University Press of Florida, 2013).

FEBRUARY 7

On February 7, 1948, the seeds of the Dixiecrat Party were sown at the Southern Governors Association conference at Wakulla Springs. At the meeting, South Carolina Governor Strom Thurmond advocated breaking off from the Democratic Party to preserve segregation and white supremacy. Thurmond feared that changes in the national Democratic Party sacrificed the South's Jim Crow norms. Thurmond ran for president as a Dixiecrat in 1948 and won a handful of southern states in the general election. The segregationist Dixiecrats only carried the states where they were listed as Democrats on the ballot. Thurmond came in a distant third in Florida, and Harry Truman secured Florida's votes and the presidency. Thurmond's decision helped break the dominance of Democrats in the South, as segregationists increasingly turned to the Republican Party to resist civil rights legislation.

FOR FURTHER READING: Kari Frederickson, *The Dixiecrat Revolt and the End of the Solid South, 1932–1968* (Chapel Hill: University of North Carolina Press, 2001).

FEBRUARY 8

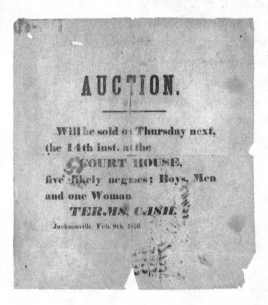

On February 8, 1856, a slave auction was advertised in Jacksonville for the following week. Set to take place at the courthouse, the advertisement boasted the sale of several unnamed enslaved people, one woman and the rest an unstated mix of men and boys. The event typified slave auctions throughout the slave South in its ability to tear apart families and operate under sanction of the courts. White owners routinely sold enslaved men and women in order to clear their debts, settle estates, as punishments, and even as a threat to free African Americans. As many as one in five children were sold away from their parents in the antebellum period. Florida was no different.

FOR FURTHER READING: Larry Eugene Rivers, *Rebels and Runaways: Slave Resistance in Nineteenth-Century Florida* (Urbana: University of Illinois Press, 2012).

FEBRUARY 9

On February 9, 1929, Ernest Hemingway wrote to his friend and fellow author John Dos Passos inviting him down to the Florida Keys to go fishing. An avid outdoorsman, Hemingway loved Florida and maintained a residence in Key West for much of the 1930s. He became a noted community fixture and wrote some of his most famous works while living in Florida, including *A Farewell to Arms* (1929), *To Have and Have Not* (1937), and part of *For Whom the Bell Tolls* (1940). Many of the characters and settings of *To Have and Have Not* were based on people and places he observed in Key West.

FOR FURTHER READING: Nancy W. Sindelar, *Influencing Hemingway: People and Places That Shaped His Life and Work* (Lanham, MD: Rowman and Littlefield, 2014).

FEBRUARY 10

On February 10, 1763, Spain ceded Florida to Britain as a condition of the 1763 treaty that ended the Seven Years' War. The year before, Spain had received the Louisiana Territory from France as part of a secret arrangement, the 1762 Treaty of Fontainebleau. That earlier treaty was designed so that France would not have to give the territory to the

victorious British and thereby allow it to expand its already large colonial holdings in North America. The 1763 treaty also forced France to
cede Canada to Britain, leaving France a handful of Caribbean islands
as its colonies in the New World.

FOR FURTHER READING: Linda Colley, *Britons: Forging a Nation, 1707–1837*
(New Haven, CT: Yale University Press, 1992).

FEBRUARY 11

On February 11, 1993, President Bill Clinton announced the nomination of Floridian Janet Reno to serve as US attorney general. Born
and raised in Miami, Reno became the first woman to hold the post.
Reno initially pursued a career in chemistry before switching to the
legal field. Despite attending Harvard University law school, she was
only able to find work at smaller firms and entered politics in the early
1970s. Reno helped reform several aspects of Florida's government before being selected as state attorney for Miami-Dade County in 1978.
The US Senate confirmed Reno's nomination on March 11, 1993, and
she served for eight years.

FOR FURTHER READING: Doris Weatherford, *They Dared to Dream: Florida
Women Who Shaped History* (Gainesville: University Press of Florida, 2015).

On February 12, 1900, "Lift Every Voice and Sing" was performed publicly for the first time at the segregated Edwin M. Stanton School in Jacksonville. The African American students at the school welcomed noted educator Booker T. Washington with the performance that was a part of a larger commemoration of Abraham Lincoln's birthday. The lyrics were written by James Weldon Johnson, Stanton's principal, and the music was written by his brother, John Rosamond Johnson. The song calls for the liberation of African Americans, combining an optimism for the future and a recognition of ongoing and past struggles. The song has since been considered the black national anthem.

FOR FURTHER READING: Imani Perry, *May We Forever Stand: A History of the Black National Anthem* (Chapel Hill: University of North Carolina Press, 2018).

James Weldon Johnson.

FEBRUARY 13

On February 13, 1960, eight Florida A&M students and two high school students went to the Woolworth's store in Tallahassee and asked to be served at its segregated lunch counter. They were inspired by civil rights activists protesting the segregation of stores and restaurants in Greensboro, North Carolina. White patrons initially continued to eat, but many left after realizing a demonstration was occurring. Other customers gathered around the students and heckled them, while one white customer offered support. The students stayed at the counter for two hours reading textbooks and left without incident or being served. With the demonstration's success, civil rights workers organized a larger sit-in for February 20 that resulted in the arrest of the protesters and attracted national attention.

FOR FURTHER READING: Glenda Alice Rabby, *The Pain and the Promise: The Struggle for Civil Rights in Tallahassee* (Athens: University of Georgia Press, 1999).

FEBRUARY 14

On February 14, 2018, a gunman opened fire at Marjory Stoneman Douglas High School in Parkland, killing seventeen people and wounding several more. The Stoneman Douglas shooting surpassed the Columbine shooting in Colorado as the deadliest high school shooting in US history. The accused gunman, Nikolas Cruz, had been expelled from the school, and his behavior had earlier raised several red flags. The local sheriff's office and the FBI received several tips about his behavior before the shooting, but they either overlooked them or found them not credible enough to justify action.

FOR FURTHER READING: Sarah Lerner, ed., *Parkland Speaks: Survivors from Marjory Stoneman Douglas Share Their Stories* (New York: Crown Books for Young Readers, 2019).

FEBRUARY 15

On February 15, 1978, authorities apprehended serial killer Ted Bundy in Pensacola for the final time. A charismatic sociopath, Bundy had been in jail several other times but had successfully eluded prosecution. On January 15, 1978, he committed two murders and assaulted three more victims at the Chi Omega sorority at Florida State

University. Bundy abducted and killed another victim in Lake City on February 9 before being captured. Bundy was convicted and sentenced to death in 1979. On death row he admitted to several other crimes. He was executed on January 24, 1989.

FOR FURTHER READING: Ann Rule, *The Stranger Beside Me* (New York: Signet, 1989).

FEBRUARY 16

On February 16, 1984, paper industry laborers testified in the trial *Winfield v. St. Joe Paper Company*. The paper company and the community of Port St. Joe became the focal point of nearly two decades of efforts to end de facto segregation and discrimination in the southern paper industry. The case was dubbed "the St. Joe saga" because of the extended time it took to settle it. Paper workers and their attorneys repeatedly returned to court to point out that the company funneled African Americans into lower-wage jobs and prevented them from advancing. The case finally ended with a consent decree in 1988.

FOR FURTHER READING: Timothy J. Minchin, *The Color of Work: The Struggle for Civil Rights in the Southern Paper Industry, 1945–1980* (Chapel Hill: University of North Carolina Press, 2001).

FEBRUARY 17

On February 17, 1793, Creek Indian leader Alexander McGillivray died in the Pensacola home and central trading house of noted merchant William Panton. Raised in and familiar with both Creek and English colonial society, McGillivray was a controversial figure who promoted

Panton home, Pensacola.

southeastern Indian interests and autonomy by pitting European colonial—and later American—governments against each other. However, he frustrated his fellow Creeks by circumventing cultural norms in attempting to centralize power under his own leadership. Toward the end of McGillivray's life, he used his political and business connections in Florida as leverage to force the US to recognize Creek interests in the Southeast.

FOR FURTHER READING: Andrew K. Frank, *Creeks and Southerners: Biculturalism on the Early American Frontier* (Lincoln: University of Nebraska Press, 2005).

FEBRUARY 18

On February 18, 1979, Richard Petty won his sixth Daytona 500 race. Petty was in a distant third on the final lap when the cars ahead of him driven by Cale Yarborough and Donnie Allison crashed into each other, allowing Petty to claim victory. As Petty took a victory lap, a fight broke out between Yarborough and Allison at the site of the wreck. The timing of the fight could not have been better for the future of NASCAR. The 1979 race was the first 500-mile race to be aired on live television. Previously, longer races were heavily edited and shown with a tape delay. The exciting finish to the race and ensuing fisticuffs helped launch NASCAR's popularity nationwide.

FOR FURTHER READING: Donnie Allison with Jimmy Creed, *Donnie Allison: As I Recall* (New York: Sports, 2013).

FEBRUARY 19

On February 19, 1968, Florida teachers went on strike to protest the lack of adequate funding needed to address the rapidly growing student population in the state's public schools. Prior to the strike, teachers and legislators recognized a crisis on the horizon. After World War II, the state's population boomed, stretching the budgets of local school boards. State lawmakers hoped to solve the issue by passing a sales tax for education in 1967. When Governor Claude Kirk vetoed the bill, teachers went on strike. Without an immediate solution, many teachers went back to work within weeks or months. Others lost their employment entirely. Eventually the state reformed education to provide for better pay and benefits but also made it illegal for state workers to go on strike.

FOR FURTHER READING: Jody Baxter Noll, "'We Are Not Hired Help': The 1968 Statewide Florida Teacher Strike and the Formation of Modern Florida," *Florida Historical Quarterly* 95, no. 3 (2017): 356–382.

FEBRUARY 20

On February 20, 1864, Confederate forces under the command of Joseph Finegan defeated the US Army at the Battle of Olustee. It was the only major battle to take place in Florida during the Civil War. Union forces under Truman Seymour advanced from Jacksonville hoping to disrupt supply lines, recruit African American allies, and potentially capture the capital city of Tallahassee. Confederate troops repelled the enemy, thereby allowing Tallahassee to remain under Confederate control. While many white Southerners hoped that news of the battle would lift spirits, the US Army maintained its advantage, and the war ended a little more than a year later.

FOR FURTHER READING: Daniel L. Schafer, *Thunder on the River: The Civil War in Northeast Florida* (Gainesville: University Press of Florida, 2010).

On February 21, 1945, Ernest Ivy Thomas Jr. assumed the platoon leadership position of a group of Marines at the base of Mount Suribachi during the Battle of Iwo Jima after his commander was wounded. Known as Boots by his fellow Marines, Thomas was born in Tampa and raised in Monticello. Two days later, Thomas was among the men who participated in the American flag raising on top of the mountain. Thomas was mortally wounded on March 3 and posthumously awarded the Navy Cross for his actions.

FOR FURTHER READING: James Bradley and Ron Connor, *Flags of Our Fathers* (New York: Bantam, 2000).

Family of Ernest Thomas, 1945.

FEBRUARY 22

On February 22, 1959, the inaugural Daytona 500 race was run in front of 41,921 fans. Lee Petty won the event after an exciting back-and-forth final lap with Johnny Beauchamp. The race was the first event held at the Daytona International Speedway, a 2.5-mile track that was the brainchild of NASCAR founder Bill France Sr. Now the Daytona 500 is the opening event and foremost race in the NASCAR season, and its location highlights Daytona Beach's and Florida's deep connections to automobile racing.

FOR FURTHER READING: Daniel S. Pierce, *Real NASCAR: White Lightning, Red Clay, and Bill France* (Chapel Hill: University of North Carolina Press, 2010).

FEBRUARY 23

On February 23, 1512, Juan Ponce de León officially received a charter to search for and explore the island of Bimini. As this was not a royally funded expedition, the royal contract set the parameters of Ponce's explorations. It gave Ponce, the former governor of Puerto Rico, the exclusive right to explore and settle nearby lands and the first rights to the labor of Native Americans. It also established the Crown's obligations to issues such as titles, tax breaks, and reimbursement for construction of necessary fortifications. The rights granted to explore and claim nearby lands were particularly important, as they established Ponce's claim to Florida.

FOR FURTHER READING: John E. Worth, *Discovering Florida: First-Contact Narratives from Spanish Expeditions along the Lower Gulf Coast* (Gainesville: University Press of Florida, 2014).

FEBRUARY 24

On February 24, 2010, Dawn Brancheau was killed by an orca at Sea-World Orlando. Brancheau was an orca trainer at the theme park. At the end of a show that day, the orca Tilikum dragged Brancheau into the water, and she drowned. Her death prompted SeaWorld to redesign its marine mammals show and led animal rights activists to protest keeping marine animals in captivity. Brancheau was not Tilikum's first victim; he had previously killed two other people in unrelated incidents. Tilikum died at the age of thirty-five in January 2017.

FOR FURTHER READING: Ed Pilkington, "Killer Whale Tilikum to Be Spared after Drowning Trainer by Ponytail," *The Guardian*, February 25, 2010.

FEBRUARY 25

On February 25, 1964, Cassius Clay defeated Sonny Liston in Miami Beach to become the world heavyweight boxing champion. The twenty-two-year-old Clay, better known by his chosen name Muhammad Ali, dominated the fight, and Liston did not answer the bell to start the seventh round. Ali soundly defeated Liston in a rematch in 1965 with a first-round knockout. Ali would go on to defend his championship several more times until he was stripped of his titles for refusing to submit to the draft during the Vietnam War.

FOR FURTHER READING: Thomas Hauser, *Muhammad Ali: His Life and Times* (London: Robson, 2004).

February 26

On February 26, 2012, seventeen-year-old African American Trayvon Martin was shot and killed by community watch member George Zimmerman. From Miami Gardens, Martin was visiting his father in Sanford when he encountered Zimmerman. Though Martin was simply walking home on a chilly night, Zimmerman reported suspicious activity to the police. Authorities instructed Zimmerman not to make contact with the young man, but Zimmerman disregarded police instructions and fatally shot Martin. Despite ignoring police instructions, Zimmerman used the controversial "Stand Your Ground" law to defend his actions. A Florida jury acquitted Zimmerman of second-degree murder charges in 2013.

FOR FURTHER READING: Christopher J. Lebron, *The Making of Black Lives Matter: A Brief History of an Idea* (New York: Oxford University Press, 2017).

February 27

On February 27, 1957, Florida officials visited Tampa and other neighboring communities at the request of citizens concerned with rising levels of air pollution. Citizens complained of various symptoms and repeatedly said their eyes and skin felt like they were burning when they were outside for a short time. They hoped they could convince the officials to help pass legislation to stop local industries from spewing chemicals into the air. Activist Harriet N. Lightfoot asked, "If this air contamination can do this to one's skin, what does it to one's lungs?" Her queries went unanswered by state and legislative officials.

FOR FURTHER READING: Scott Hamilton Dewey, "'Is This What We Came to Florida For?': Florida Women and the Fight against Air Pollution in the 1960s," *Florida Historical Quarterly* 77, no. 4 (1999): 503–531.

February 28

On February 28, 1783, Patrick Tonyn, the British governor of East Florida, learned that he had lost his job through no fault of his own. In a letter from British Secretary of State Lord Thomas Townshend, Tonyn learned about the retrocession of the colony back to Spain as part of the 1783 treaty that ended the American War of Independence. Tonyn may have lost his job, but there was still work to do. Townshend informed Tonyn that it was his obligation to tell the nearly 12,000 British residents of the area surrounding St. Augustine of the territorial cession and ask if they wanted to remain. Most of the residents evacuated by 1785.

FOR FURTHER READING: Diane Boucher, "Mayhem and Murder in the East Florida Frontier 1783 to 1789," *Florida Historical Quarterly* 93, no. 3 (2015): 446–471.

FEBRUARY 29

On Leap Day, February 29, 1864, the first integrated free school in Florida opened in Jacksonville. It was operated by the spouses of US Army officers occupying Jacksonville. Racial tensions quickly arose at the school. Although the students got along fine, white parents increasingly refused to allow their children to attend, even though it was the only opportunity for education most of them would have. As white attendance dwindled, African American pupils excelled. In the autumn of 1864, a school exclusively reserved for white students opened, and Jacksonville public schools remained officially segregated until 1970.

FOR FURTHER READING: Gerald Schwartz, "An Integrated Free School in Civil War Florida," *Florida Historical Quarterly* 61, no. 2 (1982): 155–161.

March

MARCH 1

On March 1, 1969, Floridian Jim Morrison, front man for the psyche-
delic rock band The Doors, was charged with exposing himself and
inciting a riot. The act occurred while he was onstage in Miami's Din-
ner Key Auditorium in front of 12,000 fans. Morrison attended Florida
State University in the early 1960s before becoming a rock star. The
court found Morrison guilty in September 1970 and sentenced him
to six months in jail and a $500 fine. He never served time. While he
appealed the ruling and was out on bail, he died on July 3, 1971, in
Paris. In 2007 Governor Charlie Crist suggested that Morrison receive
a posthumous pardon, which was granted in December 2010.

FOR FURTHER READING: Stephen Davis, *Jim Morrison: Life, Death, Legend*
(New York: Gotham, 2005).

MARCH 2

On March 2, 1954, the Florida Seminoles protested the termination of their tribal status before a joint congressional committee in Washington, DC. The federal government pursued the termination policy in an effort to cut expenditures to Indians nationwide and otherwise force the assimilation of Indigenous people. During the two days of testimony, the Seminoles insisted that they had a right to maintain their tribal status but also that they would not be a public charge for long. Laura Mae Osceola, when asked by a committee member if she thought extending Seminole recognition for twenty-five years would make a difference, defiantly declared that soon Seminoles "won't need your help. We will be giving you help." Osceola's statement foreshadowed an era of economic and political development for the Seminoles in which they negotiated with state, local, and federal officials to sell tax-free products on reservations and pioneer tribal gaming nationwide.

FOR FURTHER READING: Harry A. Kersey Jr., *An Assumption of Sovereignty: Social and Political Transformation among the Florida Seminoles, 1953–1979* (Lincoln: University of Nebraska Press, 1996).

MARCH 3

On March 3, 1845, Florida became the twenty-seventh state to enter the United States. The path to statehood was slow, as Florida's population remained too small to meet congressional mandates. White Floridians held a constitutional convention and applied for statehood anyway. Congress ignored the request for many years. Its ultimate success had more to do with the strength of Iowa's claims than with its own merits. When the territory of Iowa pursued statehood, southern congressmen backed Florida's application in order to maintain the balance of power between slave and free states. The *Pensacola Gazette* explained the connection best when it stated, "Florida and Iowa are Siamese twins—one cannot go without the other."

FOR FURTHER READING: Stephanie D. Moussalli, "Florida's Frontier Constitution: The Statehood, Banking, and Slavery Controversies," *Florida Historical Quarterly* 74, no. 4 (1996): 423–439.

Act establishing Florida statehood, 1845.

MARCH 4

On March 4, 1824, territorial Governor William Pope Duval proclaimed Tallahassee to be the capital of the territory of Florida. After Spain ceded Florida to the United States in 1821, the territorial legislature alternated its meetings between St. Augustine and Pensacola. However, travel between the two population centers was long and difficult. Leaders of each of those dueling capitals of what were once East Florida and West Florida refused to allow the other town to become the permanent location, and a compromise was born. They chose Tallahassee, an old Indian field and village, because it was roughly the midpoint between the two towns and had good access to fresh water.

FOR FURTHER READING: Stephanie D. Moussalli, "Florida's Frontier Constitution: The Statehood, Banking, and Slavery Controversies," *Florida Historical Quarterly* 74, no. 4 (1996): 423–439.

MARCH 5

On March 5, 1946, Jackie Robinson fled the small town of Sanford when local white inhabitants threatened him with violence. Robinson had gone to Sanford to participate in spring training with the Brooklyn Dodgers. Robinson, who would break the color barrier in Major League Baseball in 1947, was assigned to the Dodgers' minor league affiliate, the Montreal Royals, for the 1946 season. Segregation laws prevented Robinson from staying at the same hotel as the rest of the team, and instead he stayed at the home of a local middle-class African American family. This did not satisfy the local white community members who opposed the integration of baseball and Robinson's presence in their midst. The Dodgers subsequently established their own facility in Vero Beach to avoid racist resistance to Robinson and other African American players.

FOR FURTHER READING: Chris Lamb, *Blackout: The Untold Story of Jackie Robinson's First Spring Training* (Lincoln: University of Nebraska Press, 2006).

JACKIE ROBINSON

Says:

Don't Buy Discrimination!

*Hear Jackie Robinson speak in honor of the
18 CORE members jailed for being
"undesirable" at a lunch counter.*

**8 P.M.   Greater Bethel
Thursday, A. M. E. Church
Sept. 1st   245 N.W. 8th St.**

Miami CORE - Congress of Racial Equality

1960

Flier for Jackie Robinson's appearance at the Greater Bethel A.M.E. Church in Miami on September 1, 1960.

MARCH 6

On March 6, 1865, Confederate volunteers, mostly teenagers and men too old to enlist, successfully repelled a larger US Army force at the Battle of Natural Bridge near modern-day Woodville outside Tallahassee. One of the last Confederate victories of the Civil War, the battle made Tallahassee the only Confederate capital to not fall during the war. The US Army made few attempts to capture the small and distant capital during the war, and American soldiers easily occupied Tallahassee on May 10. Further, with Florida effectively blockaded and several of the coastal areas occupied, Tallahassee's lack of real strategic value as a target during the Civil War contributed to the capital city's historic distinction.

FOR FURTHER READING: David J. Coles, "Florida's Seed Corn: The History of the West Florida Seminary during the Civil War," *Florida Historical Quarterly* 77, no. 3 (1999): 283–319.

March 7

On March 7, 1935, Malcolm Campbell of England broke his own land speed record at Daytona Beach. Driving his car Blue Bird, Campbell reached a speed of 276 miles per hour. Daytona Beach was the preferred location for speed runs until technology allowed speeds that necessitated even longer tracks. Campbell's record from March 7 was the last one in Florida. Campbell and others moved to Utah's Bonneville Salt Flats, which boasts nearly fourteen uninterrupted miles.

FOR FURTHER READING: J. A. Martin and Thomas F. Saal, *American Auto Racing: The Milestones and Personalities of a Century of Speed* (Jefferson, NC: McFarland, 2004).

March 8

On March 8, 1669, a Spanish government official in St. Augustine wrote to the queen of Spain regarding his worries about English pirates attacking coastal settlements. Those fears increased in the wake of the 1668 Searles Raid in which pirates sacked St. Augustine. The official wrote requesting more soldiers and more money from the Spanish Crown to protect Florida from additional pirate attacks that he feared were imminent. As a result of the official's repeated letters, the Spanish built the Castillo de San Marcos. The fort still stands and is run by the National Park Service.

FOR FURTHER READING: Diana Reigelsperger, "Pirate, Priest, and Slave: Spanish Florida in the 1668 Searles Raid," *Florida Historical Quarterly* 92, no. 3 (2014): 577–590.

March 9

On March 9, 1861, large-scale cotton planters in Florida, Georgia, and Alabama petitioned the Confederate government for assistance. When the war began, many planters remained committed to growing cotton instead of food and other essential crops. The US Navy's seemingly impenetrable blockade of the port of Apalachicola cut them off from this formerly lucrative trade and access to the basic necessities that it provided. Some blockade runners successfully bypassed the naval blockade elsewhere during the war, but few attempted to get to the Gulf port. As a result, even the wealthiest slaveholders often dealt with hunger and other deprivations.

FOR FURTHER READING: Maxine Turner, *Navy Gray: A Story of the Confederate Navy on the Chattahoochee and Apalachicola Rivers* (Tuscaloosa: University of Alabama Press, 1988).

March 10

On March 10, 1998, federal governmental weather forecasters predicted a continuation of the unusual El Niño weather pattern that had begun the previous summer. The 1997–1998 El Niño event led to a significant outbreak of tornadoes in February that resulted in forty-two deaths across Florida. In June and July 1998, wildfires fueled by the drought associated with the weather pattern destroyed millions of dollars' worth of personal and agricultural property in the Sunshine State.

FOR FURTHER READING: Stanley A. Changnon, ed., *El Niño 1997–1998: The Climate Event of the Century* (New York: Oxford University Press, 2000).

March 11

On March 11, 1811, Governor William C. C. Claiborne of the Orleans Territory raised troops to put down a revival of the West Florida rebellion against the Spanish. President James Madison saw the revolt as an opportunity to seize West Florida. The white residents of West Florida, who were mostly American settlers along with land speculators eager to see the territory added to the United States, proclaimed the area the free Republic of West Florida. The republic was bounded by the Mississippi River and present-day Mobile, Alabama. Ironically, the Republic of West Florida did not have any land in modern-day Florida.

FOR FURTHER READING: Samuel C. Hyde, "Introduction: Setting a Precedent for Regional Revolution; The West Florida Revolt Considered," *Florida Historical Quarterly* 90, no. 2 (2011): 121–132.

MARCH 12

On March 12, 1956, the US Supreme Court ruled that the University of Florida law school had to admit forty-five-year-old Virgil Hawkins. The Florida Supreme Court led by Justice B. K. Roberts continued to prevent Hawkins from attending the school and altered the requirements for entry so that Hawkins no longer qualified. Hawkins subsequently attended an unaccredited law school and was admitted to practice law in Florida in 1977. Florida State University later named its law school for Roberts, the justice who led the fight to keep Hawkins out of UF.

FOR FURTHER READING: Judith G. Poucher, *State of Defiance: Challenging the Johns Committee's Assault on Civil Liberties* (Gainesville: University Press of Florida, 2014).

MARCH 13

On March 13, 1812, a group of around seventy men styling themselves "Patriots" and seeking annexation into the United States assembled at Rose's Bluff on the St. Marys River in northeastern Florida. With support from the United States, the Patriots seized Amelia Island on March 17 and used it as a base of operations over the next two years.

The Patriot Constitution of 1812.

Of the men at Rose's Bluff, fewer than ten were actually from Florida. Many of the anti-Spanish belligerents in the ensuing Patriot War were American citizens who hoped their efforts could help the United States extend its territory. After writing a constitution to set up local law, many "patriots" assumed the United States would quickly annex the new republic. It, along with the rest of Florida, would not become part of the United States until 1821.

FOR FURTHER READING: James G. Cusick, *The Other War of 1812: The Patriot War and the American Invasion of Spanish East Florida* (Gainesville: University Press of Florida, 2003).

MARCH 14

On March 14, 1903, President Theodore Roosevelt established the Pelican Island National Wildlife Refuge, the first federal bird reservation for the conservation of unique bird species. Located just east of Sebastian, the refuge was designed to preserve egrets and other birds from threats of extinction caused by a fashion-inspired plume trade. The global demand for white egret feathers ultimately inspired one of the nation's first conservation movements. Pelican Island was one of fifty-one such bird reserves that Roosevelt created during his time in office. It became a National Historic Landmark in 1963.

FOR FURTHER READING: Edmund Morris, *Theodore Rex* (New York: Modern Library, 2001).

MARCH 15

On March 15, 1738, Governor Manuel Montiano granted freedom and citizenship to enslaved people from Carolina in return for their militia service to Spain and fidelity to the Crown. The freed people subsequently established Gracia Real de Santa Teresa de Mosé just north of St. Augustine. Mosé's inhabitants played important roles in the defense of Florida during English raids, and its very existence encouraged enslaved men and women in South Carolina and Georgia to seek freedom in Florida.

FOR FURTHER READING: Jane Landers, *Black Society in Spanish Florida* (Urbana: University of Illinois Press, 1999).

MARCH 16

On March 16, 1943, the US and Bahamian governments reached the first agreement that established the British West Indies Temporary Labor Program; the second such agreement was made between the United States and Jamaica on April 2. Florida was by far the largest recipient of West Indian laborers, men and women who mostly worked in seasonal agricultural jobs like cutting sugarcane. The program began as a stop-gap measure to replace the large numbers of American workers who joined the military or worked in the war manufacturing industry during World War II. The program ended in 1947, but Florida employers continued to hire British West Indies agricultural laborers through the H2-A visa program.

FOR FURTHER READING: Terry L. McCoy and Charles H. Wood, *Caribbean Workers in the Florida Sugar Cane Industry* (Gainesville: University of Florida Center for Latin American Studies, 1982).

MARCH 17

On March 17, 1960, eleven civil rights protesters had their day in a Tallahassee courtroom stemming from their involvement in the February sit-ins at the Woolworth lunch counter restaurant. All were found guilty and ordered to pay $300 fines or serve sixty days in jail. Eight of the protesters chose jail over bail and began their sentences at the Leon County jail on March 18. Although the nonviolent sit-ins were originally conceived in North Carolina, civil rights workers in Florida were the first to decide to serve their jail time rather than pay the fines. The decision brought a great deal of attention to the injustices of southern segregation.

FOR FURTHER READING: Glenda Alice Rabby, *The Pain and the Promise: The Struggle for Civil Rights in Tallahassee* (Athens: University of Georgia Press, 1999).

From: CORE - Congress of Racial Equality
        Roosevelt Hotel, St. Louis, Missouri

        Attn: Marvin Rich

FOR RELEASE: Wednesday evening, June 29, 1960

        FIVE JAILED STUDENT LEADERS GIVEN GANDHI AWARD BY CORE

        Five jailed student leaders received CORE's Gandhi Award
at a mass meeting opening CORE's 18th Annual Conference-
Convention in St. Louis today.

        The five--Barbara and John Broxton, William Larkins,
Patricia and Priscilla Stephens--received the award for their
outstanding contributions during the year in improving race
relations through direct, nonviolent methods.

        Rev. Wyatt Tee Walker, himself jailed for sitting-in at a
Petersburg, Virginia public library, presented the Gandhi Award
to the young leaders.

                        Sacrificed Selves

        The citation says: "They spent 49 days in a Florida jail
for 'disturbing the peace and public tranquility' by sitting
quietly at a Woolworth lunch counter. They chose to serve a
jail sentence rather than pay an unjust fine. Later they were
asked by University officials to withdraw from school for a
semester. They have sacrificed themselves for the right as they
saw it.

        "Under their leadership the Tallahassee CORE group has
sustained a direct action program. This deep South group has
been thoroughly interracial and has managed to increase its
membership and influence in the community, in spite of attacks
from politicians and white citizens council elements.

        "The five leaders have borne abuse and contumely with
restraint and dignity. They have maintained a spirit of good
will and of understanding. They have not swerved from the
objective of equal rights for all."

        All the students have been placed on probation by Florida
A. & M. University for their role in leading the sit-ins. CORE
will assist the students in securing their education during the
coming school year.

CORE press release honoring five FAMU students among the jailed protesters.

March 18

On March 18, 2005, Terri Schiavo's feeding tube was removed for the last time. Schiavo had been in a persistent vegetative state since 1990 after a heart attack led to massive brain damage and coma. Her case gained notoriety when her legal guardian/husband and her parents disagreed about what Schiavo's end-of-life wishes would have been. Her husband asserted that she would not have wanted to live in a vegetative state, but legal motions from Schiavo's parents caused significant delays in the case as Florida's governor, the Florida legislature, and US Congress, as well as local, state, and federal courts, became involved in the Schiavo case. The case became a landmark in right-to-die and living-will cases. Schiavo died on March 31.

FOR FURTHER READING: Kenneth W. Goodman, *The Case of Terri Schiavo: Ethics, Politics, and Death in the 21st Century* (New York: Oxford University Press, 2010).

March 19

On March 19, 2018, Governor Rick Scott signed legislation removing the statue of Edmund Kirby Smith from the National Statuary Hall. Smith was a Confederate general who had also served in the US Army and fought in the Mexican-American War. Smith was not an especially successful general for the Confederates, failing to relieve the Union siege of Vicksburg, Mississippi, in 1863. Florida officials chose to replace the Smith statue with one of African American educator and civil rights activist Mary McLeod Bethune.

FOR FURTHER READING: Karen Cox, *Dixie's Daughters: The United Daughters of the Confederacy and the Preservation of Confederate Culture* (Gainesville: University Press of Florida, 2019).

March 20

On March 20, 1984, the City of Fort Lauderdale passed a series of ordinances designed to end the city's central place in the nation's spring break scene for college students. For decades, thousands of students from across the nation descended on the city each year, temporarily turning the beachside community into a world-renowned party scene. Spring break business was good for some, but many residents and business owners declared that the college students degraded the town's image as a tourist destination. Students, the protesters complained, spent far less money than older and less rowdy visitors, as students

predominantly frequented fast-food places and beachside bars. The complaints led the city to make itself less hospitable to underage drinking by cracking down on public intoxication and overcrowded hotels. The new ordinances worked. Within a few years, Fort Lauderdale lost most of its spring break business to other towns in Florida and beyond.

FOR FURTHER READING: James Schlitz, "Time to Grow Up: The Rise and Fall of Spring Break in Fort Lauderdale," *Florida Historical Quarterly* 93, no. 2 (2014): 195–225.

Spring Break in Daytona Beach,
ca. 1980s.

March 21

On March 21, 1940, the Alfred Hitchcock film *Rebecca* premiered in Miami. Starring Laurence Olivier and Joan Fontaine, the movie was based on Daphne du Maurier's gothic novel. The movie focuses on the second wife of a rich widower who was trying to outlive the memory of his deceased wife, a woman who died tragically at sea but whose presence remains everywhere in the de Winter house. In this psychological thriller, the presence of Rebecca continues thanks to the efforts of the devoted but sinister housekeeper, Mrs. Danvers. The film won two Academy Awards, including Best Picture, in 1941. *Rebecca* was Hitchcock's first American-made film and his only film to win Best Picture.

FOR FURTHER READING: Leonard Leff, *The Rich and Strange Collaboration of Alfred Hitchcock and David O. Selznick in Hollywood* (Berkeley: University of California Press, 1999).

MARCH 22

On March 22, 1691, the Spanish explorer Andrés de Pez delivered his report to the king of Spain's Junta de Guerra on the benefits of reestablishing a permanent Spanish colony at Pensacola Bay. Pez hoped to build his new town on the very site of a 1559 colony that ended after only two years. He proposed that doing so would create a deterrent to rival colonial powers in the area. Pez had initially been tasked with locating the French explorer La Salle's expedition in modern-day Texas. Instead, they stumbled upon the excellent deep-water bay along the way. Though the junta was unimpressed with his reasoning, Pez's arguments convinced Charles II to reestablish a colony at Pensacola Bay by building a new presidio there that the Spanish named Santa María de Galve.

FOR FURTHER READING: Judith A. Bense, "Presidio Santa María de Galve (1698–1719): A Frontier Garrison in Spanish West Florida," *Historical Archaeology* 38 (2004): 3–14.

MARCH 23

On March 23, 1840, General Zachary Taylor wrote to territorial Governor Robert R. Reed to express his displeasure at the ineffectiveness of bloodhounds in tracking down the enemy during the Second Seminole War. As the US military struggled to track the enemy in the southern Florida wetlands, officials authorized the purchase of tracking

HUNTING INDIANS IN FLORIDA WITH BLOOD HOUNDS.

dogs from Cuba to aid in the war effort. Abolitionists and critics of the war decried the use of bloodhounds as dehumanizing and a symbol of the immoral means by which the nation defended the institution of slavery. The dogs were largely ineffective at any rate, and political cartoonists lampooned the Army's efforts.

FOR FURTHER READING: John Campbell, "The Seminoles, the 'Bloodhound War,' and Abolitionism, 1796–1865," *Journal of Southern History* 72, no. 2 (2006): 259–302.

MARCH 24

On March 24, 1942, Ted W. Lawson and other pilots took off from Eglin Field (now Eglin Air Force Base) near Pensacola en route to California and the USS *Hornet*. Flying in their B-25 Mitchell bombers, the Air Force pilots had just completed training in Florida, where they perfected flying medium-range bombers off the decks of Navy aircraft carriers. A month later they would participate in the Doolittle Raid, a

mission planned by Lieutenant Colonel Jimmy Doolittle to attack Tokyo in response to the Pearl Harbor attack.

FOR FURTHER READING: Ted W. Lawson and Bob Considine, *Thirty Seconds
over Tokyo* (New York: Random House, 1943).

MARCH 25

On March 25, 1822, Lieutenant Matthew C. Perry—the same naval officer who later opened Japanese trading markets to the rest of the world
through the 1854 Kanagawa Convention—sailed the USS *Shark* to Key
West and claimed the island as an American territory. After the transfer of Florida to the United States, Spain maintained that the Keys
were part of Cuba and therefore not subject to the Adams-Onís Treaty.
Realizing the island's strategic importance, Perry planted an American
flag on Key West to claim it as part of the United States. Perry was part
of a larger US naval squadron tasked with fighting rampant smuggling
and piracy in the Caribbean.

FOR FURTHER READING: John C. Fredriksen, *The United States Navy: A
Chronology, 1775 to the Present* (Santa Barbara, CA: ABC-CLIO, 2010).

MARCH 26

On March 26, 1886, Ignacio Haya opened his first cigar factory in
modern-day Ybor City. The factory opened the year after a fire destroyed much of Key West's cigar-making industry. Haya was alerted
to the plentiful and cheap land on the outskirts of Tampa by his friend
and rival Vicente Martinez Ybor, who was also setting up his new cigar
factory there. The creation of the cigar-making industry in Ybor City
transformed this section of Tampa and made it the heart of a vibrant
Cuban immigrant community.

FOR FURTHER READING: Durward Long, "The Historical Beginnings of Ybor
City and Modern Tampa," *Florida Historical Quarterly* 45, no. 1 (1966): 31–44.

MARCH 27

On March 27, 1513, Juan Ponce de León first sighted Florida after sailing from Puerto Rico and the Bahamas in search of the island of Bimini. Ponce and his sailors mistakenly believed the land to be an island. Ponce named the area La Florida because of the verdant nature of its landscape and because spring is the season of what the Spanish call "the festival of flowers" (*pascua florida*). Historians still debate exactly where the Spaniards landed, with many different places given as possibilities. Most scholars contend that he landed on the Atlantic coast of northern Florida, somewhere south of current-day St. Augustine.

FOR FURTHER READING: Samuel Turner, "Juan Ponce de León and the Discovery of Florida Reconsidered," *Florida Historical Quarterly* 92, no. 1 (2013): 1–31.

MARCH 28

On March 28, 1568, Spanish explorer Pedro Menéndez Márquez sent a letter from Havana to Spanish authorities describing attacks by the Tequesta of southeastern Florida on the Spanish garrison at Tocobaga. Both attacks occurred on what is now called Mound Key in Lee County. When the Spanish sailed to the area, they confronted the gruesome reality that nearly everybody in the Tocobaga garrison was either dead or missing as a result of a Tequesta attack. Márquez wrote that the few survivors made their way to the Spanish fort San Antón de Carlos, where they were starving as a result of a lack of provisions.

FOR FURTHER READING: John E. Worth, *Discovering Florida: First-Contact Narratives from Spanish Expeditions Along the Lower Gulf Coast* (Gainesville: University Press of Florida, 2014).

MARCH 29

On March 29, 2001, the Florida legislature approved House Bill 1083, introduced to restrict access to autopsy photographs in the wake of

racing driver Dale Earnhardt's death in the 2001 Daytona 500. This law, commonly referred to as the Earnhardt Family Protection Act, limits access to postmortem examination photos. Earnhardt's widow, Teresa, provided the impetus for the bill over concerns that under Florida's broad public records laws any person could request and publish images of her dead husband. Several groups unsuccessfully challenged the law on the basis that it limited access to records and went against the intent of Florida's sunshine laws.

FOR FURTHER READING: Clay Calvert, "A Familial Privacy Right over Death Images: Critiquing the Internet-Propelled Emergence of a Nascent Constitutional Right That Preserves Happy Memories and Emotions," *Hastings Constitutional Law Quarterly* 40 (2013): 475–523.

MARCH 30

On March 30, 1822, the United States formally established the territory of Florida by combining East and West Florida. This marked the culmination of a long-cherished dream held by American expansionists who wanted to incorporate Florida into the nation. Spain agreed in 1819 to cede its Florida colonies to America, after finding them to be an increasing burden on exhausted Spanish resources. The United States officially took over the colonies in 1821 and organized them as a single territory in 1822. Americans had been settling illegally in Florida during Spain's colonization, and the US Army made frequent incursions into Spanish Florida to wage war on Seminoles who attacked settlers in Georgia.

FOR FURTHER READING: Allen Morris and Amelia Rea Maguire, "The Unicameral Legislature in Florida," *Florida Historical Quarterly* 58, no. 3 (1980): 303–314.

MARCH 31

On March 31, 1880, William H. Hunt of the Life-Saving Service wrote to his supervisor about the quarterly estimate needed for the houses of refuge program along Florida's eastern coast. At the end of the nineteenth century, most of the Atlantic coastline remained largely unoccupied by white settlers. As a result, shipwrecked sailors often died of starvation or thirst before they could be rescued. Under the program the refuge houses provided shelter for shipwreck victims as well as homes for lighthouse keepers and bases for life-saving crews.

FOR FURTHER READING: Sandra Henderson Thurlow, "Lonely Vigils: Houses of Refuge on Florida's East Coast, 1876–1915," *Florida Historical Quarterly* 76, no. 2 (1997): 152–173.

THE WRECK.

APRIL 1

On April 1, 1865, Florida Governor John Milton committed suicide rather than live with what he considered the indignity of reuniting with the United States at the conclusion of the Civil War. Milton entered the governor's office in October 1861. Though few battles occurred in Florida early in the Civil War and Florida had a very small population, Milton pushed Florida to become important to the Confederacy's war efforts through supplying food and salt to the Southern army. With his public reputation tied to the ultimate failure of the Confederacy, Milton chose death rather than dishonor. Abraham K. Allison took over as governor after Milton's suicide.

FOR FURTHER READING: Sean Patrick Adams, "Patriotism Derailed: John Milton, David Yulee, and the Florida Railroad in 1863," *Florida Historical Quarterly* 86, no. 3 (2008): 406–416.

APRIL 2

On April 2, 1513, Juan Ponce de León claimed Florida for Spain. The king of Spain told Ponce prior to his expedition that he would become a lifelong governor of any lands he discovered, but Ponce had to pay all of the expenses associated with the journey. He landed somewhere along Florida's northeastern coast between St. Augustine and Melbourne Beach with approximately 200 men and three ships. After some brief exploration of the area for visible gold or silver deposits, Ponce and his crew left the area to sail farther south. Though popular legend has it that Ponce was searching for the fountain of youth, that myth was created and propagated many years later.

FOR FURTHER READING: Samuel Turner, "Juan Ponce de León and the Discovery of Florida Reconsidered," *Florida Historical Quarterly* 92, no. 1 (2013): 1–31.

APRIL 3

On April 3, 2006, the University of Florida men's basketball team won the NCAA tournament. Under the direction of head coach Billy Donovan, the Gators defeated the UCLA Bruins by a final score of 73–57, securing UF's first-ever college basketball championship. The Gators became one of only seven programs to repeat tournament championships 364 days later, defeating Ohio State University. Under Billy Donovan, the Gators posted an impressive 467–186 record between 1996 and 2015.

FOR FURTHER READING: John Grasso, *Historical Dictionary of Basketball* (Lanham, MD: Scarecrow, 2010).

APRIL 4

On April 4, 1923, the Tamiami Trail Blazers led by Russell Kay, a local businessman, began their automotive trek across the largely uncharted Everglades from Fort Myers to Miami. Henry Ford, Thomas Edison,

and other celebrities attended the launch party, bringing national notoriety to the first attempt to cross the southern Florida Peninsula by car. Their trip was supposed to last only three days, but the Trail Blazers were reported lost on April 8 after they failed to reach Miami on the appointed day. With the help of Seminole Indian guides, they eventually made it to their end destination nineteen days after they left Fort Myers.

FOR FURTHER READING: Russell Kay, "Tamiami Trail Blazers: A Personal Memoir," *Florida Historical Quarterly* 49, no. 3 (1971): 278–287.

APRIL 5

On April 5, 1800, William Augustus Bowles declared war against Spain on behalf of the State of Muskogee. Bowles was an Englishman born in colonial Maryland and served in the British army during the Revolutionary War until he was kicked out for insubordination. Following

this disgrace, Bowles migrated south, eventually arriving in Indian lands north of Pensacola. There, he married a Lower Creek woman, the daughter of an influential village leader. Through his connections he was able to wield considerable influence among the Creeks and attract disaffected white and black Floridians to his cause.

FOR FURTHER READING: J. Leitch Wright Jr., *William Augustus Bowles: Director General of the Creek Nation* (Athens: University of Georgia Press, 2010).

APRIL 6

On April 6, 1927, the *Maitland News* published a memorial to Lida Bronson, a longtime Florida Audubon Society member. Bronson earned prominence by fighting to preserve native Florida bird species when their plumes were in great demand in the women's fashion industry. She served as the treasurer of the Florida Audubon Society, one of the first women to become a leader in the conservation group. The craze for bird plumes led to the extinction of several bird species and dramatic population decreases in others.

FOR FURTHER READING: Leslie Kemp Poole, "The Women of the Early Florida Audubon Society: Agents of History in the Fight to Save State Birds," *Florida Historical Quarterly* 85, no. 3 (2007): 297–323.

APRIL 7

On April 7, 1896, the railroad tracks from Henry Morrison Flagler's Florida East Coast Railroad reached Miami. Flagler had agreed to extend his railroad to Miami after the Great Freeze of 1895 hit northern Florida and killed citrus trees throughout the state. Flagler had discussed the possibility of extending the railroad to the southern tip of Florida for many years but worried that he would not recoup his costs. When the citrus groves in southern Florida were spared from the freeze, a gift of citrus blossoms from Miamian Julia Tuttle changed his mind. Flagler's decision to extend the railroad down to Miami essentially led to its incorporation and growth, making Miami "the city that Flagler built."

FOR FURTHER READING: Andrew K. Frank, *Before the Pioneers: Indians, Settlers, Slaves, and the Founding of Miami* (Gainesville: University Press of Florida, 2017).

APRIL 8

On April 8, 1927, the Florida Theatre opened in Jacksonville. At the time, it was the largest theater in the state of Florida. It had the capability of showing films and newsreels, and it was large enough to offer live entertainment on its stage. Elvis Presley famously played at the Florida Theatre in 1956, attracting the attention of local authorities who warned him that he risked arrest if he performed any gyrations. The Florida Theatre was added to the National Register of Historic Places in 1982.

FOR FURTHER READING: Shawn C. Bean, *The First Hollywood: Florida and the Golden Age of Silent Filmmaking* (Gainesville: University Press of Florida, 2008).

APRIL 9

On April 9, 1988, the fiftieth anniversary of the publication of *The Yearling* was celebrated at the Marjorie Kinnan Rawlings State Historic Site in Cross Creek. Folk singers Will McLean and Cousin Thelma Boltin performed, with singer-songwriter Gamble Rogers joining them to sing "Oklawaha County Laissez-Faire." Rawlings's 1938 coming-of-age story focuses on the love of a rural Florida boy and his orphaned fawn. It was later made into an Oscar-nominated film starring Gregory Peck and Jane Wyman.

FOR FURTHER READING: Bruce Horovitz, *Gamble Rogers: A Troubadour's Life* (Gainesville: University Press of Florida, 2018).

APRIL 10

On April 10, 1874, author Harriet Beecher Stowe met Governor Marcellus Stearns on the Tallahassee Capitol steps, where she was photographed along with black and white leaders. Stowe was surprised at the reception she received from white Floridians because of her strong abolitionist beliefs and the infamy that *Uncle Tom's Cabin* earned her prior to the Civil War. Local white Floridians took her on multiple garden tours and even had a gala reception thrown in her honor. Stowe

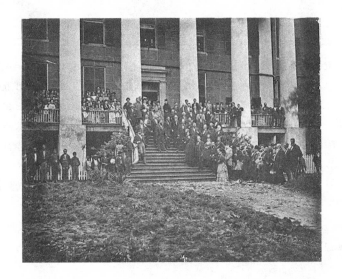

was a frequent Florida visitor, spending much of her time in St. Augustine. On one occasion, she rented Laurel Grove, the cotton plantation formerly owned by Zephaniah Kingsley. Her *Palmetto Leaves* reflects her experiences and impressions of her time in Florida.

FOR FURTHER READING: T. D. Allman, *Finding Florida: The True History of the Sunshine State* (New York: Atlantic Monthly, 2013).

APRIL 11

On April 11, 1862, General R. F. Floyd suggested that Governor John Milton proclaim martial law in certain eastern Florida counties in order to prevent a slave uprising. At the start of the Civil War, many enslaved African Americans fled in acts of self-emancipation. To Floyd's surprise, many white Floridians made little effort to prevent further escapes. Raising a militia, Floyd suggested, was the only way to prevent a total uprising. During the war, thousands of enslaved Floridians used the turmoil of the Civil War to reunite with loved ones, enlist in the US Army, and find freedom.

FOR FURTHER READING: David Williams, *I Freed Myself: African American Self-Emancipation in the Civil War Era* (New York: Cambridge University Press, 2014).

APRIL 12

On April 12, 1981, the inaugural launch of the *Columbia* initiated NASA's space shuttle program. The *Columbia* was designed to be a reusable spacecraft that could transport heavy loads to a space station. *Columbia* played an important role in the program, as it took twenty-eight missions into space. On February 1, 2003, it disintegrated upon reentry. All seven crew members died. It was later determined that a piece of debris struck the shuttle during launch, damaging a wing and the thermal protection necessary for reentry.

FOR FURTHER READING: Margaret A. Weitekamp, "Selling Education in the Shape of a Shuttle," *Florida Historical Quarterly* 87, no. 2 (2008): 210–234.

APRIL 13

You Can't Fool Mother Nature

STOP ERA

Equal Rights Amendment

STOP ERA IN FLORIDA
A SPECIAL PROJECT OF
THE CONSERVATIVE CAUCUS, INC.
7777 Leesburg Pike
Falls Church, Virginia 22043

On April 13, 1977, the Florida Senate voted 21–19 against ratifying the Equal Rights Amendment (ERA) resolution. The ERA elicited heated debate about whether an amendment should be added to the US Constitution to grant equal rights to women and end legal distinctions between men and women. After passing through both houses of the US Congress and being sent to individual states for ratification, the proposed amendment stalled in the divided political environment of Florida. It failed due to its being portrayed as an attack on traditional gender roles and values, especially in religious circles. In large part because of resistance in the South, the amendment has not passed.

FOR FURTHER READING: Laura E. Brock, "Religion and Women's Rights in Florida: An Examination of the Equal Rights Amendment Legislative Debates, 1972–1982," *Florida Historical Quarterly* 94, no. 1 (2015): 1–39.

APRIL 14

On April 14, 1836, Brevet Brigadier General Duncan L. Clinch and his column left Tampa during the early months of the Second Seminole War. The US military advance was in some disarray as it suffered from outbreaks of several infectious diseases and shortages of food, ammunition, and other supplies. Clinch left nearly 10 percent of his command behind in sick quarters at Tampa and headed off to relieve another unit stationed at a blockhouse fort on the Withlacoochee River. Clinch's frustrations with the fighting conditions and irregular warfare in Florida typified those of other officers in the long war with the Seminoles.

FOR FURTHER READING: Matthew T. Pearcy, "'The Ruthless Hand of War': Andrew A. Humphreys in the Second Seminole War," *Florida Historical Quarterly* 85, no. 2 (2006): 123–153.

APRIL 15

On April 15, 1980, the Mariel boatlift began. The exodus out of Cuba began when the Cuban government granted permission to leave the island to anyone seeking asylum in foreign embassies if the countries

were willing to grant entry. Most of the immigrants left from Mariel Harbor, leading to the name "marielitos" for those who made the journey. President Jimmy Carter announced that the United States would accept 3,500 refugees, though more than 100,000 Cubans ultimately arrived in America by way of Miami before the boatlift was ended by both governments in October 1980. The Cuban arrivals overwhelmed authorities in South Florida, resulting in the construction of temporary tent cities.

FOR FURTHER READING: Kate Dupes Hawk, Ron Villella, Adolfo Leyva de Varona, and Kristen Cifers, *Florida and the Mariel Boatlift of 1980: The First Twenty Days* (Tuscaloosa: University of Alabama Press, 2014).

APRIL 16

On April 16, 1886, a few dozen captive Chiricahua Apaches were taken to St. Augustine for imprisonment in the Castillo de San Marcos. The small band of Apaches, among them Geronimo, had surrendered to US troops in Arizona before being sent on to Florida. More than 500 Apaches would ultimately spend time in the St. Augustine prison. The fort was not designed to hold much more than 100 prisoners, and many died in the overcrowded conditions. The Apaches were held in St. Augustine before being eventually removed to Fort Sill, Oklahoma. Many of the captured children were forcibly removed from their parents' care and sent to Carlisle Indian Industrial School in Pennsylvania to be assimilated into white society.

FOR FURTHER READING: Robert M. Utley, *Geronimo* (New Haven, CT: Yale University Press, 2012).

APRIL 17

On April 17, 1785, Florida Governor Arturo O'Neill reported that bandits from Georgia were crossing the porous border into East Florida to steal horses, livestock, and slaves. O'Neill complained to Spanish officials that he was powerless to stop Georgians from ravaging the Spanish settlements along the St. Marys River. Additional difficulties ensued when Georgians stole from Seminole Indians, which threatened to bring warfare to the region. The difficulties that O'Neill described reveal the contentious nature of the Florida borderlands as a place occupied by many but not really controlled by anyone.

FOR FURTHER READING: Diane Boucher, "Mayhem and Murder in the East Florida Frontier, 1783 to 1789," *Florida Historical Quarterly* 93, no. 3 (2015): 446–471.

APRIL 18

On April 18, 1832, abolitionist and educator Chloe Merrick was born near Syracuse, New York. Merrick married future Florida governor Harrison M. Reed in 1869; they had met at the interracial school where she taught on Amelia Island. She founded an orphanage in 1863 on the island after discovering a large number of needy children. By 1865 the orphanage housed fifty children. The following year Merrick contracted malaria, and her poor health forced her to close her orphanage. In the years that followed, she continued to reform, often through her husband's position, Florida's educational system and otherwise alleviate poverty in the state.

FOR FURTHER READING: Sarah Whitmer Foster and John T. Foster, "Chloe Merrick Reed: Freedom's First Lady," *Florida Historical Quarterly* 71, no. 3 (1993): 279–299.

APRIL 19

On April 19, 1656, Spanish Governor Diego de Rebolledo ordered members of the Timucua, Apalachee, and Guale militia to report to the presidio at St. Augustine for a month's service. Rebolledo raised the force in response to the British attack on Jamaica the year before.

Rebolledo also commanded the militia to each carry seventy-five pounds of corn to the fort, as there were ongoing food shortages in the capital. The Native chiefs deemed Rebolledo's order to be an insult to their distinguished place in Indigenous communities and blind to the food shortages their own people were enduring. In response to his high-handed demands, the Timucua rose up in rebellion against the Spanish, only to be suppressed by an expedition of Spanish troops and Guale soldiers led by Rebolledo. In November 1656 the Spanish convicted ten chiefs and sentenced them to death for their rebellious actions.

FOR FURTHER READING: John E. Worth, *The Timucuan Chiefdoms of Spanish Florida: Resistance and Destruction*, 2 vols. (Gainesville: University Press of Florida, 1998).

APRIL 20

On April 20, 2010, the Gulf of Mexico oil drilling platform Deepwater Horizon in the Macondo Prospect suffered a catastrophic failure. The result was the worst offshore spill in history. Approximately 4.9 billion barrels spilled; eleven workers were killed, and seventeen others were injured in the explosion. It is believed that defective cement along the wall that resulted from cost-cutting decisions made by British Petroleum and its partners caused the explosion. Although BP agreed to pay nearly $19 billion in fines and pled guilty to eleven counts of manslaughter, the ecological and economic impact of the oil spill is still being measured years later.

FOR FURTHER READING: Republic of the Marshall Islands Office of the Maritime Administrator, "Deepwater Horizon Marine Casualty Investigation Report," Official Report no. 2213, August 17, 2011.

APRIL 21

On April 21, 1899, the *Miami Metropolis* announced that the W. S. Davis family was preparing to leave the Peacock Inn in Cocoanut Grove after their visit. (Cocoanut Grove would standardize its spelling as

Coconut Grove when it incorporated in 1919.) One of the first hotels in South Florida, the Peacock Inn was founded in 1882, and it catered to tourists who wanted to escape winter weather in the north. Local and national newspapers reported visitors' comings and goings in their society pages to attract newcomers and otherwise promote the region. The marketing worked, as South Florida's population swelled during the winter tourist season. The Peacock Inn became famous after it was featured in Caroline Washburn Rockwood's *In Biscayne Bay*, a popular novel about South Florida published in 1891.

FOR FURTHER READING: Susannah Worth, "The Peacock Inn: South Florida's First Hotel," *Florida Historical Quarterly* 91, no. 2 (2012): 151–180.

APRIL 22

On April 22, 2000, on the orders of US Attorney General Janet Reno, FBI agents took Elián González from his Miami family members to return him to his father in Cuba. Four hours later he was returned to his father's custody. González's parents were divorced after he was born, and when he was five, his mother, Elizabeth Brotons Rodriguez, along with twelve other Cuban refugees, attempted to reach the United States by boat. Elizabeth and ten others died at sea when the boat's motor failed and a storm swamped the craft. Local fishermen rescued the survivors off the coast of Miami and turned them over to the Coast Guard. González became embroiled in a custody battle between his Cuban father and American relatives until US officials determined that his father should be his guardian as opposed to his extended American family in Miami.

FOR FURTHER READING: Antonio Rafael de la Cova, "The Elián González Case: The World's Most Watched and Politically Charged Custody Battle That Reached the US Supreme Court and Determined a Presidential Election," *Harvard Latino Law Review* 18 (2015): 151–200.

On April 23, 1982, the Conch Republic in Key West jokingly seceded from the United States. The spoof underlined serious issues residents had with the US government. Earlier in 1982, the Border Patrol set up a roadblock on US 1 where it stopped all cars to check for the presence of narcotics or illegal immigrants. The Key West City Council fought the roadblock in court, claiming that it deterred tourists and inconvenienced residents. Seeing the roadblock as a sort of border crossing, the council said it was as if Key West was a foreign country and proclaimed its independence. It declared the sand dollar to be the currency of the republic, even as it continued to accept American dollars.

FOR FURTHER READING: William C. Barnett, "Inventing the Conch Republic: The Creation of Key West as an Escape from Modern America," *Florida Historical Quarterly* 88, no. 2 (2009), 139–172.

APRIL 24

On April 24, 1898, the US War Department selected Tampa its main mobilization site for the Spanish-American War. It chose Tampa because of the town's proximity to the Caribbean, deep-water port, and access to modern railways. An estimated 66,000 US soldiers came through Tampa en route to the war in Cuba and Puerto Rico. The US government spent approximately $4 million on the war, mostly in Tampa. Prior to the outbreak of the war, Tampa had a population of around 17,000, making it the third largest in Florida at the time, but with the influx of soldiers and civilians working toward the war effort, the population swelled to more than 37,000 in 1910. The wartime growth cemented Tampa's future as a major city in Florida.

FOR FURTHER READING: Spencer Tucker, ed., *The Encyclopedia of the Spanish-American and Philippine-American Wars: A Political, Social, and Military History*, vol. 1. Santa Barbara, CA: ABC-CLIO, 2009.

APRIL 25

On April 25, 1928, the Tamiami Trail officially opened, connecting Tampa to Miami with a paved road for the first time. At the time, Miamians supported the venture more than residents of Tampa, which already had many connections to the rest of the state. It was built from 1915 to 1928, required more than 2.6 million sticks of dynamite, and ultimately cost approximately $8 million. The road proved ecologically devastating to the Everglades. A series of dams and other forms of water control resulted in parts of the River of Grass drying up. Since the 1990s, the Army Corps of Engineers has, with mixed success, tried to address the problem.

FOR FURTHER READING: Tamiami Trail Commissioners and County Commissioners of Dade County, Florida. *History of the Tamiami Trail: And a Brief Review of the Road Construction Movement in Florida* (Miami: Tamiami Trail Commissioners and County Commissioners of Dade County, Florida, 1928).

APRIL 26

On April 26, 1860, the Cuban slave ship *Wildfire* was captured off the shore of Key West by the US Navy steamer *Mohawk*. Aboard the ship were 507 enslaved Africans bound for Cuba and the rapidly expanding sugar industry there. A total of 615 Africans had been originally captured from near the Congo River before the survivors were forced aboard the *Wildfire*. The *Wildfire* was part of a larger effort to violate the ban on the transatlantic slave trade. It was one of three slave ships captured and taken to Key West by the Navy that month; the two others had a total of more than 1,400 enslaved Africans on board. All the

captains and crews were tried by the US government for participating in the illegal Atlantic slave trade, but none were convicted.

FOR FURTHER READING: Larry Eugene Rivers, *Slavery in Florida: Territorial Days to Emancipation* (Gainesville: University Press of Florida, 2008).

APRIL 27

On April 27, 1962, the US Air Force Special Air Warfare Center opened at Eglin Air Force Base. Its primary purpose was to assist in counterinsurgency operations. It was established during the Cold War, specifically during the Vietnam War, continued through the US invasion of Panama in 1989–1990, and lasted through Operation Desert Storm in the Persian Gulf region in 1990–1991. Established in 1935, Eglin AFB is a focal point of all Air Force armaments, operating as an Air Force materiel command. The base orchestrates, conducts, and directs the testing and evaluation of all US air armaments as well as navigation and guidance systems.

FOR FURTHER READING: John C. Fredriksen, *The United States Air Force: A Chronology* (Santa Barbara, CA: ABC-CLIO, 2011).

APRIL 28

On April 28, 1988, President Ronald Reagan signed into law the Abandoned Shipwreck Act. It stipulates that any submerged wrecks found in a state's waters belonged to the state. As a result of the new law,

Florida began to develop the Underwater Preserves, a chain of twelve sites that people equipped with scuba gear may visit free of charge any day of the year. Each of the sites has a plaque explaining its historical significance and relevant features. Only six other US states have underwater resources similar to Florida's Underwater Preserves.

FOR FURTHER READING: Steven D. Singer, *Shipwrecks of Florida* (Sarasota: Pineapple Press, 1998).

APRIL 29

On April 29, 1818, General Andrew Jackson had British citizens Alexander George Arbuthnot and Robert C. Ambrister executed on charges that they helped the Creek and Seminole Indians during the ongoing First Seminole War. Jackson had invaded Spanish Florida to harass and hunt down defiant Native Americans. During the invasion Arbuthnot and Ambrister were found at a Spanish fort in present-day Bay County. Earlier in April, Jackson's men captured several enemy Creeks, including Josiah Francis (Hillis Hadjo) and Homathlemico, and executed them without trial. In response to Jackson's illegal actions, Congress found some fault with both British men's trials and the way Jackson handled the executions, but it decided against censuring him.

FOR FURTHER READING: Deborah Rosen, *Border Law: The First Seminole War and American Nationhood* (Cambridge, MA: Harvard University Press, 2015).

On April 30, 1562, Jean Ribault, a French navigator and colonizer, explored the St. Johns River. He did so to find an adequate location to begin a settlement with the 150 Frenchmen he brought with him. Ribault claimed the land for France, erected a stone column, and ultimately established a settlement on Parris Island in modern-day South Carolina. Ribault named the site Charlesfort in honor of the French king Charles IX. Charlesfort soon fell into disrepair. A few survivors attempted to return to France, but most perished on the crossing. Ribault decided that a new settlement should be established farther south, leading to the establishment of Fort Caroline on the banks of the St. Johns in northeastern Florida.

FOR FURTHER READING: Chuck Meide and John de Bry, "The Lost French Fleet of 1565: Collision of Empires," in 2014 *Underwater Archaeology Proceedings*, ed. Charles Dagneau and Karolyn Gauvin, 79–92 (Rockville, MD: Advisory Council on Underwater Archaeology, 2014).

May

MAY 1

On May 1, 1946, the *St. Petersburg Times* chose not to endorse two-term Florida House member Mary Lou Baker. She was the second woman elected to the Florida legislature when she won office in 1942, and she was reelected in 1944. Instead of endorsing the wartime representative, the *Times* endorsed a man in large part because of his gender. In their explanation, the editors explained that Baker failed to live up to various campaign promises, and they declared that it would be  a liability for a woman to serve. Like other women who stepped into new roles in employment and government during World War II, Baker was expected to return to domestic life after the war.

FOR FURTHER READING: Doris Weatherford, *They Dared to Dream: Florida Women Who Shaped History* (Gainesville: University Press of Florida, 2015).

MAY 2

On May 2, 1957, Governor LeRoy Collins issued a statement against Florida House Concurrent Resolution No. 174, one of many legislative efforts designed to resist *Brown v. Board of Education* and racial integration. The statement was commonly called the interposition statement; through HCR 174 legislators attempted to "interpose" the state between the federal government and the people of Florida to prevent public school integration. Collins opposed state resistance on this matter to the outrage of many southern Democrats. Collins, who could not veto House resolutions, hand-wrote his disapproval on the official document, noting, "I want it known that I did my best to avert this blot."

FOR FURTHER READING: Martin A. Dyckman, *Floridian of His Century: The Courage of Governor LeRoy Collins* (Gainesville: University Press of Florida, 2006).

MAY 3

On May 3, 1901, the Great Fire left 10,000 residents homeless when it devoured much of Jacksonville, the largest city in Florida at the time. The conflagration began at the Cleveland Fiber Factory when embers from a small fire ignited Spanish moss that was being laid out to dry. Workers tried to put out the flames, but the city had been suffering

from a drought, and the predominantly wooden structures stood little chance. The fire blazed for at least eight hours, and the glow from the conflagration was reported to be seen as far away as Savannah, Georgia. The fire consumed nearly 150 city blocks and 2,400 buildings.

FOR FURTHER READING: Louis Zelenka, "Telegraphic Correspondence Relating to the Jacksonville Fire of 1901," *Florida Historical Quarterly* 80, no. 2 (2001): 225–234.

MAY 4

On May 4, 1858, Billy Bowlegs and his band of Seminoles departed South Florida on the steamer *Grey Cloud*. They were bound for their new home in Indian Territory, modern-day Oklahoma, at the end of the Third Seminole War. The captured Seminoles included Madeloyee, a woman widely known as Polly Parker. She and her Seminole husband, Chai, had worked as guides for the US Army during the Seminole Wars. When the ship stopped for provisions in St. Marks, Parker escaped when she was allowed to disembark to collect herbs and other supplies. She made her way back to South Florida, where she lived until 1921. Today, many members of the Seminole Tribe of Florida attribute their subsequent survival in Florida to Parker's courageous escape.

FOR FURTHER READING: Laurel Clark Shire, *The Threshold of Manifest Destiny: Gender and National Expansion in Florida* (Philadelphia: University of Pennsylvania Press, 2016).

On May 5, 1961, astronaut Alan Shepard's spacecraft took off from Cape Canaveral, and he thereby became the first American to be launched into space. Shepard barely missed the honor of being the first human in space; he was edged out by Soviet cosmonaut Yuri Gagarin on April 12, 1961. Shepard's flight on the *Freedom 7*, a Mercury spacecraft, lasted a brief fifteen minutes before the craft splashed down in the Atlantic Ocean. Shepard later became the fifth and also the oldest person to walk on the moon, where he famously hit two golf balls while on the lunar surface.

FOR FURTHER READING: Neal Thompson, *Light This Candle: The Life and Times of Alan Shepard, America's First Spaceman* (New York: Crown, 2004).

MAY 6

On May 6, 1851, physician John Gorrie received a patent for his ice machine. Born in the West Indies and raised in South Carolina, Gorrie moved to Apalachicola in the early 1830s. As a medical doctor, he focused on relieving sufferers of tropical diseases and used ice to cool rooms as an early form of air conditioning. This method required large

quantities of ice, prompting Gorrie to abandon the medical field and focus on his invention. He never received sufficient financial support for his efforts and died insolvent in 1855. His contributions to artificial cooling were important enough for Gorrie to be represented among Florida's figures in the National Statuary Hall.

FOR FURTHER READING: Jonathan Rees, *Refrigeration Nation: A History of Ice, Appliances, and Enterprise in America* (Baltimore, MD: Johns Hopkins University Press, 2013).

MAY 7

On May 7, 1943, Draper L. Kauffman was picked to lead the under-water demolition team training at the Amphibious Scout and Raider School at Fort Pierce. The US Army initially constructed Fort Pierce during the Second Seminole War because of its easy access for supply ships on the coast and expeditions designed to forcibly remove Semi-noles from the interior. The Army reoccupied the fort more than a century later for its proximity to the Atlantic coast. Fort Pierce was selected by the US military because the area could be used to mimic the beaches in the European and Pacific theaters during World War II. Beaches around Fort Pierce had fortifications built on them for sol-diers to learn how best to breach and then remove them. Kauffman's underwater demolition teams were the forerunner of the modern Navy SEALs.

FOR FURTHER READING: Nick Wynne and Richard Moorhead, *Florida in World War II: Floating Fortress* (Charleston, SC: Arcadia, 2011).

MAY 8

On May 8, 1865, the East Gulf Blockading Squadron of the US Navy captured the Confederate vessel *George Douthwaite*. The ship was car-rying sugar, rum, wool, and ginger from Jamaica. The USS *Isonomia* captured the ship off the Warrior River in West Florida; it was the last blockade runner the US Navy captured during the Civil War. The East Gulf was one of four US blockade squadrons created at the start of the Civil War. Each was tasked with cutting off shipping to and from Confederate ports. The East Gulf was responsible for blockading the Florida Peninsula from Cape Canaveral to St. Andrew Bay in the Gulf of Mexico. During its three and a half years of service, the East Gulf Blockading Squadron captured or destroyed nearly 300 vessels, most of which were attempting to reach Apalachicola.

FOR FURTHER READING: David J. Coles, "Unpretending Service: The *James L. Davis*, the *Tahoma*, and the East Gulf Blockading Squadron," *Florida Historical Quarterly* 71, no. 1 (1992): 41–62.

May 9

On May 9, 1980, the Sunshine Skyway Bridge in Tampa Bay collapsed. The disaster occurred when a freight ship collided with two of the bridge's support piers during a sudden, unforecasted storm. The MV *Summit Venture* crew briefly lost radar during the storm and struggled to navigate through torrential rains and winds that approached 70 miles per hour. Thirty-five people died when the southbound span collapsed and a Greyhound bus and other vehicles fell into Tampa Bay 150 feet below. More than 1,200 feet of the bridge fell into the water after the impact. After the accident, the remaining section of the southbound bridge was converted into a fishing pier. A new Sunshine Skyway Bridge opened on April 20, 1987.

FOR FURTHER READING: William Leonard DeYoung, *Skyway: The True Story of Tampa Bay's Signature Bridge and the Man Who Brought It Down* (Gainesville: University Press of Florida, 2013).

May 10

On May 10, 1865, the US Army occupied Tallahassee. It had been the only Confederate capital east of the Mississippi not to have been captured during the war. Tallahassee was threatened a few times during the war, most notably at the Battle of Natural Bridge in March 1865. After the surrender of Southern troops in April, the US Army under Brigadier General Edward McCook with a modest force entered Tallahassee and occupied the capital city. This occupation was accompanied by similar occupying forces throughout the South moving into politically strategic and symbolic areas. US troops would remain in Florida and the South until 1877.

FOR FURTHER READING: David J. Coles, "Florida's Seed Corn: The History of the West Florida Seminary during the Civil War," *Florida Historical Quarterly* 77, no. 3 (1999): 283–319.

May 11

On May 11, 1996, ValuJet Flight 592 crashed into the Everglades after taking off from Miami International Airport. All 110 passengers died. Before the accident, the flight to Atlanta had been delayed due to mechanical problems, but the cause of the disaster was later determined to have been a fire that started in the cargo area below the passenger cabin. Investigators found that more than 100 expired chemical oxygen generators were placed in the cargo hold against Federal Aviation Administration regulations. ValuJet had a poor safety record prior to the May 11 crash, and the FAA grounded the airline for several months afterward. The company name later was changed to AirTran Airlines. Southwest Airlines eventually acquired the company and dropped the AirTran name.

FOR FURTHER READING: Roger W. Cobb and David M. Primo, *The Plane Truth: Airline Crashes, the Media, and Transportation Policy* (Washington, DC: Brookings Institution Press, 2004).

May 12

On May 12, 1955, Florida Attorney General Richard Ervin submitted an amicus brief to the US Supreme Court in response to the *Brown v. Board of Education* ruling. In the brief he advocated for gradual integration, as *Brown* did not include any method of ending racial segregation in schools or a timeline for when that would occur. Because of the ambiguity, southern states obtained flexibility with which to resist school integration. To counteract the desire of southern legislators to resist, delay, and otherwise fight integration, the US Supreme Court issued a ruling known as *Brown II* on May 31, 1955. The court found that integration should proceed "with all deliberate speed."

FOR FURTHER READING: Glenda Alice Rabby, *The Pain and the Promise: The Struggle for Civil Rights in Tallahassee* (Athens: University of Georgia Press, 1999).

MAY 13

On May 13, 1954, LeRoy Collins read from a May 14 issue of the *Miami Herald* during a televised debate with acting Governor Charlie Johns. The newspaper, printed hours before the gubernatorial candidate debate occurred, claimed that Johns had won the debate even though it had not yet taken place. Johns had become governor with the passing of Governor Dan McCarty in September 1953 in accordance with the state constitution's succession plan, which stated that the Senate president took on the position until a special election could take place. The premature editorial embarrassed Johns's already struggling campaign. Collins won the 1954 special election and was reelected in 1956.

FOR FURTHER READING: Martin A. Dyckman, *Floridian of His Century: The Courage of Governor LeRoy Collins* (Gainesville: University Press of Florida, 2006).

MAY 14

On May 14, 2008, the demolition of the Orange Bowl in Miami was completed. The historic football stadium, originally built in 1937 and named Burdine Stadium for one of Miami's pioneers, hosted the Orange Bowl game from 1938 to 1996 and again in 1999. The stadium also served as the University of Miami's home game site through the

2007 season. The bowl game and the Hurricanes had relocated to what is now Hard Rock Stadium on a permanent basis as the Orange Bowl's facilities became outdated. Through its lifetime, the Orange Bowl, as it was renamed in 1959, hosted five Super Bowls as well as many baseball games, concerts, boxing events, and soccer matches.

FOR FURTHER READING: Marty Strasen, *Canes vs. Gators: Inside the Legendary Miami Hurricanes and Florida Gators Football Rivalry* (New York: Sports, 2016).

MAY 15

On May 15, 1699, Governor of Florida Don Laureano de Torres y Ayala penned a letter to the viceroy of Mexico informing him of English intrigue in Florida and the Gulf Coast. His concern over outsider interference in the region became magnified when an English ship sank off the coast of St. Augustine. Shipwreck survivors told their Spanish guards that the English planned to establish a settlement on "Apalachee Bay." The location in question was actually Tampa Bay, revealing the English unfamiliarity with Florida coasts. After this incident, Torres sent an expedition from St. Augustine to the region to see if the English had landed there in defiance of Spanish claims to the entire Florida Peninsula. The expedition discovered that the English had been in the area but left before the Spanish arrived.

FOR FURTHER READING: Ronald Wayne Childers, "Historic Notes and Documents: A Late Seventeenth-Century Journey to Tampa Bay," *Florida Historical Quarterly* 80, no. 4 (2002): 504–522.

MAY 16

On May 16, 1979, civil rights leader Asa Philip Randolph died in New York at the age of ninety. Randolph was born in Crescent City, Florida, in 1889; his family moved to Jacksonville in 1891. Although he was educated and talented in various ways, Randolph realized he would be barred from all but menial jobs in Florida. As a young adult he moved to New York City to pursue other opportunities. He became a union

organizer and met with great success as the president of the Brother-
hood of Sleeping Car Porters, which he helped create as a union for
the mostly black workers. He became involved with the civil rights
movement shortly thereafter and participated with Martin Luther King
Jr. in the March on Washington for Jobs and Freedom in 1963.

FOR FURTHER READING: Andrew E. Kersten and Clarence Lang, eds.
*Reframing Randolph: Labor, Black Freedom, and the Legacies of A. Philip
Randolph* (New York: New York University Press, 2015).

MAY 17

On May 17, 1777, the Battle of Thomas Creek occurred between British
loyalists called the King's Carolina Rangers and Georgia Continental
soldiers in northern East Florida. The battle was one of three that took
place during America's failed attempt to seize East Florida from British hands. The British forces led by Thomas Brown were composed of
British regulars, loyalists, and Native American allies. The British am-
bushed and overwhelmed the Continentals, who panicked and broke
lines in a disorderly retreat. As many as eight Americans were killed
and around thirty were taken prisoner in the attack. About half the
prisoners were killed by their Native American captors. The British
forces suffered no casualties.

FOR FURTHER READING: Edward J. Cashin, *The King's Ranger: Thomas Brown
and the American Revolution on the Southern Frontier* (Athens: University of
Georgia Press, 1989).

MAY 18

On May 18, 1955, Mary McLeod Bethune passed away in Daytona
Beach. Bethune was born in 1875 in South Carolina. Her parents had
been enslaved. Bethune focused on getting an education so she could
become a missionary. She began teaching in her home state before
moving to Florida, where she opened a school for African American
girls in 1904. The school eventually merged with an all-male school to

become Bethune-Cookman College. Later in life Cookman became a spokesperson for civil and women's rights and was an adviser to President Franklin Delano Roosevelt.

FOR FURTHER READING: Audrey Thomas McCluskey and Elaine M. Smith, eds., *Mary McLeod Bethune, Building a Better World: Essays and Selected Documents* (Bloomington: Indiana University Press, 2001).

MAY 19

On May 19, 1946, the *Palm Beach Post* reported that a local group asked local officials to take care of the city's solid waste problem as a means to ameliorate the polio epidemic. At the time, it was not yet known that polio spread through infected feces. Many Americans feared contagion from the open burning of garbage, a practice that caused other health issues. The campaign against the burning of waste led residents to confront one of the problems brought on by the postwar population boom in South Florida.

FOR FURTHER READING: Andrew Fairbanks, Jennifer Wunderlich, and Christopher Meindl, "Talking Trash: A Short History of Solid Waste Management in Florida," *Florida Historical Quarterly* 91, no. 4 (2013): 526–557.

On May 20, 1865, the first Emancipation Day was held to celebrate the end of slavery in the United States. Ten days after Tallahassee was taken from the Confederates on May 10, 1865, a Union officer, General Edward McCook, read the Emancipation Proclamation from the steps of a downtown house to an assembled crowd. The house has since been converted to the Knott House Museum. There, every year on May 20, a reenactor reads the Emancipation Proclamation to commemorate the occasion.

FOR FURTHER READING: Allen Morris and Joan Perry Morris, eds., *The Florida Handbook, 2011–2012*, 33rd biennial edition (Tallahassee: Peninsular, 2011).

May 21

On May 21, 1865, the Reverend W. J. Ellis of St. John's Episcopal Church in Tallahassee neglected to include the prayer for the health of the president of the United States in his sermon. This omission came on the heels of the fall of the Confederacy and the occupation of the capital by US forces. Ellis was reprimanded by the recently arrived commander of the Union army in Tallahassee. US General Edward McCook told Ellis that if the omission occurred again or if Ellis fomented discord, Union forces would shut down the church.

FOR FURTHER READING: Lee L. Willis, "Secession Sanctified: Bishop Francis Huger Rutledge and the Coming of the Civil War in Florida," *Florida Historical Quarterly* 82, no. 4 (2004): 421–437.

MAY 22

On May 22, 1966, Louise Rebecca Pinnell died at the age of eighty-nine. Born on March 31, 1877, Pinnell was the first female attorney in Florida. Her path to becoming an attorney was fraught with public debate. The Florida Supreme Court deliberated from May to October 1898 about whether to admit her to the bar. The court then subjected Pinnell to a rigorous oral bar exam that many believed was devised to discourage women  from pursuing a career in law. It did not deter Pinnell. She passed the exam and practiced law in Northeast Florida for sixty years.

FOR FURTHER READING: Doris Weatherford, *They Dared to Dream: Florida Women Who Shaped History* (Gainesville: University Press of Florida, 2015).

MAY 23

On May 23, 1992, Ruby McCollum died. She was a wealthy African American woman from Live Oak who was incarcerated and then confined to a mental hospital for more than twenty years. She served time in local jails and Florida State Hospital, a psychiatric facility in Chattahoochee. McCollum was tried in 1952 for the murder of a white doctor she claimed had repeatedly raped her and forced her to carry his children when she became pregnant. McCollum was found guilty by an all-white jury after the court prevented her from introducing evidence that showed that the abuse was long-standing and that she had acted in self-defense. McCollum initially received the death penalty, but the Florida Supreme Court dismissed the verdict on a procedural issue. McCollum was subsequently deemed unfit to stand trial and committed to the state mental hospital, where she lived for the next twenty years. In 1974 her attorney proved that McCollum was not a danger to herself or others, and she was released. Zora Neale Hurston witnessed McCollum's first trial and publicized the case throughout the country.

FOR FURTHER READING: Tammy Evans, *The Silencing of Ruby McCollum: Race, Class, and Gender in the South* (Gainesville: University Press of Florida, 2006).

MAY 24

On May 24, 1818, General Andrew Jackson captured Pensacola without a fight after he invaded Spanish West Florida to attack Creek and Seminole Indians. Jackson contended that President James Monroe had implied permission to chase the Spanish from Florida, but he was only authorized to prevent Florida from becoming a refuge for runaway slaves. Jackson and US Secretary of State John Quincy Adams argued that if the United States held a large chunk of Florida, Spain would be more likely to relinquish control of the territory to the United States. Jackson's actions complicated Adams's negotiations with Spain, but they ultimately did not prevent the transfer of Florida to the United States in the Adams-Onís Treaty.

FOR FURTHER READING: John K. Mahon, "The First Seminole War, November 21, 1817–May 24, 1818," *Florida Historical Quarterly* 77, no. 1 (1998): 62–67.

MAY 25

On May 25, 1539, Hernando de Soto landed nine ships with more than 600 men and 200 horses on the shores near Tampa Bay. Along with his soldiers, Soto also brought settlers and craftsmen. The purpose of Soto's expedition was twofold: to locate and mine gold and silver and to begin colonization of La Florida. After the landing, Soto led an expedition north into the modern-day US Southeast, where he interacted and largely fought with Native American communities they encountered. Soto died of a fever on May 21, 1542, on the banks of the Mississippi River. The exact location of his burial remains unknown.

FOR FURTHER READING: Charles M. Hudson, *Knights of Spain, Warriors of the Sun: Hernando de Soto and the South's Ancient Chiefdoms* (Athens: University of Georgia Press, 1997).

MAY 26

On May 26, 1956, the Tallahassee bus boycott began when police arrested two African American college students for sitting in white-only seats on a city bus. The arrest of Wilhelmina Jakes and Carrie Patterson spurred fellow students at Florida A&M University to orchestrate a boycott that spread beyond the college community. Instead of taking city buses, African Americans offered transportation to those who needed it with private taxi services and other forms of ride sharing. By summer the boycott worked and city buses were effectively integrated.

FOR FURTHER READING: Glenda Alice Rabby, *The Pain and the Promise: The Struggle for Civil Rights in Tallahassee* (Athens: University of Georgia, 1999).

MAY 27

Map of St. Augustine, 1589.

On May 27, 1586, Sir Francis Drake, as ordered by Queen Elizabeth I of England, arrived in St. Augustine on the return voyage of his attack on Spanish colonies. He decided to seize the settlement the following day. Drake burned the little settlement to the ground on May 29. Spanish Governor Pedro Menéndez Marqués had already evacuated the colony after receiving a warning from officials in Santo Domingo that Drake was on his way north. After sacking St. Augustine, Drake sailed on to the English colony at Roanoke, which he provisioned, and then returned back to England. Drake's actions so angered Spanish King Philip II that he ordered a retaliatory invasion of England by the Spanish Armada.

FOR FURTHER READING: Harry Kelsey, *Sir Francis Drake, the Queen's Pirate* (New Haven, CT: Yale University Press, 1998).

MAY 28

On May 28, 1938, James Bailey Cash Jr. was kidnapped from his parents' Princeton, Florida, home. The kidnapping of five-year-old "Skeegie," as his parents called him, quickly gained national attention and drew comparisons to the infamous Lindbergh baby kidnapping. FBI Director J. Edgar Hoover personally helped investigate the case. Despite ransom payments by Skeegie's father, kidnapper Franklin Pierce McCall murdered the young boy. McCall was executed at Raiford prison on February 24, 1939.

FOR FURTHER READING: Robert A. Waters and Zack C. Waters, *The Kidnapping and Murder of Little Skeegie Cash: J. Edgar Hoover and Florida's Lindbergh Case* (Tuscaloosa: University of Alabama Press, 2014).

MAY 29

On May 29, 1776, British regulars began assembling on the banks of the St. Marys River in East Florida, where they awaited orders from General Charles Cornwallis to join the southern expedition during the American Revolution. The Georgia militia fought several skirmishes and eventually pushed the British back to the St. Johns River in the eastern part of the territory. During the war, East Florida was mostly composed of British loyalists and enslaved Africans, and it therefore did not join the thirteen colonies that became the United States.

FOR FURTHER READING: Roger Smith, "The Failure of Great Britain's 'Southern Expedition' of 1776: Revisiting Southern Campaigns in the Early Years of the American Revolution, 1775–1779," *Florida Historical Quarterly* 93, no. 3 (2015): 387–414.

MAY 30

On May 30, 1688, María Josepha and Simón José were baptized in St. Augustine. The event is significant because they had escaped enslavement in the Carolinas and made their way south to Spanish Florida. Upon arrival in Florida, they quickly learned that if they became Catholics the Spanish would protect them from being repatriated to slavery. As a result, a significant number of free African Americans held a prominent place in seventeenth- and eighteenth-century St. Augustine.

FOR FURTHER READING: Susan Richbourg Parker, "St. Augustine in the Seventeenth Century: Capital of La Florida," *Florida Historical Quarterly* 92, no. 3 (2014): 554–576.

MAY 31

On May 31, 1866, John Ringling, the best known of the seven Ringling brothers, was born in Iowa. Ringling and his brothers became famous for their eponymous circus, which essentially helped make the circus what it became in its twentieth-century heyday. The Ringlings began their show in 1870, and by 1892 it was large enough to require transporting the production on trains as opposed to animal-drawn wagons. In 1909 the brothers bought Barnum and Bailey's Greatest Show on Earth and became America's "Circus Kings." John and his wife, Mable, began spending winters, the season the circus did not travel, in Sarasota. There they eventually purchased large tracts of land and built a mansion and art museum on the land. He was the longest-living of

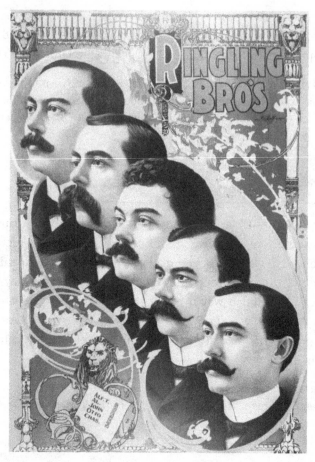

the Ringling brothers, dying in 1936 at the age of seventy. He left his thirty-room mansion, museum, and large art collection to the state of Florida. The Ringling circus lasted until 2017.

FOR FURTHER READING: David Chapin Weeks, *Ringling: The Florida Years, 1911–1936* (Gainesville: University Press of Florida, 1993).

June

JUNE 1

On June 1, 1937, Amelia Earhart and navigator Fred Noonan took off from Miami on the ill-fated attempt at a round-the-world flight. Arriving in Miami from Oakland, California, the pair hoped to finish

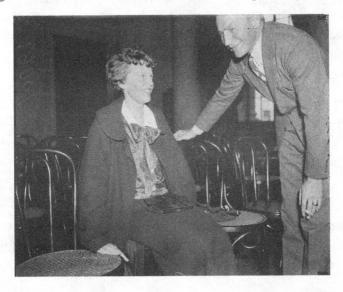

circumnavigating the globe by flying east. Over the next month, Earhart and Noonan made several flights in their Lockheed Electra, stopping in South America, Africa, southern Asia, and Australia. Earhart and Newnan were lost over the Pacific on July 2, leaving an unsolved mystery of their fate and numerous theories trying to solve the puzzle.

FOR FURTHER READING: Susan Butler, *East to the Dawn: The Life of Amelia Earhart* (Cambridge, MA: Da Capo, 1997).

JUNE 2

On June 2, 1971, the Florida Senate debated whether to enact the Florida Mental Health Act, better known as the Baker Act. The act allows for involuntary examination and institutionalization in a mental health facility for individuals believed to be suffering from mental illness or deemed a threat to themselves or others. People may be detained up to seventy-two hours if deemed necessary by a judge, physician, mental health professional, or law enforcement officer. The governor signed the bill on June 15, 1971. The act is named after Maxine Baker, the Democratic state representative from Miami who sponsored the bill. Baker made mental health a priority throughout her time in the legislature.

FOR FURTHER READING: *History of the Baker Act: Its Development and Intent* (Tallahassee: Mental Health Program Office, Florida Department of Children and Families, 2002).

JUNE 3

On June 3, 1961, Clarence Earl Gideon was arrested in Panama City for burglary and larceny. Gideon was poor and could not pay for his own legal representation. He asked the trial court for a public defender, but the court maintained that attorneys were only provided for indigent defendants in capital cases. Without counsel, Gideon was found guilty and sentenced to five years in prison. However, he successfully appealed his case all the way to the US Supreme Court, which ruled in his favor on March 18, 1963. *Gideon v. Wainwright* established the precedent that the US Constitution guaranteed a right to counsel for the accused.

FOR FURTHER READING: Anthony Lewis, *Gideon's Trumpet* (New York: Vintage, 1989).

JUNE 4

On June 4, 1939, the *St. Louis*, a German passenger ship carrying more than 900 Jewish refugees fleeing from Nazi persecution, approached Miami after leaving Cuba. The ship was denied permission to dock in Cuba and attempted to land in the United States. Authorities once again turned the ship away despite the efforts of some of President Franklin Roosevelt's cabinet to persuade him otherwise. Canada also rejected the entry of the *St. Louis*. All of its passengers were forced to return to Europe, where it is estimated that one quarter of them died in Nazi death camps.

FOR FURTHER READING: Sarah A. Ogilvie and Scott Miller, *Refuge Denied: The* St. Louis *Passengers and the Holocaust* (Madison: University of Wisconsin Press, 2006).

JUNE 5

On June 5, 1865, John C. Breckinridge, former Confederate secretary of war and former US vice president, attempted to flee from Miami to the Bahamas after the dissolution of the Confederacy by President Jefferson Davis. Breckinridge and several other Confederates tried to escape capture by Union forces they presumed would arrest and try them for treason. However, the original lifeboat proved to be too small, forcing the band of fugitives to hijack a larger vessel with a mast and rigging that would be more seaworthy for the journey. They recompensed the craft's owners by giving them the lifeboat and $20 in gold coinage. The group eventually reached Cuba but only after surviving two storms at sea and a pirate attack.

FOR FURTHER READING: Andrew K. Frank, *Before the Pioneers: Indians, Settlers, Slaves, and the Founding of Miami* (Gainesville: University Press of Florida, 2017).

JUNE 6

On June 6, 1898, at his Tampa headquarters, General Nelson A. Miles received the final plans for the joint US-Cuban Liberation Army attack on Santiago, Cuba. Miles opposed the war; he argued that the situation between America and Spain could be resolved diplomatically. Miles did not play much of a role in the invasion of Cuba as commanding general of the US Army. Instead, he organized a successful attack on Puerto Rico that led to the island's annexation to the United States. In addition to his service in the Spanish-American War, Miles is also remembered for his role in US military actions against Native Americans such as personally accepting the surrenders of several famous Native chiefs including Sioux Chief Sitting Bull and Nez Perce Chief Joseph.

FOR FURTHER READING: Spencer Tucker, ed., *The Encyclopedia of the Spanish-American and Philippine-American Wars: A Political, Social, and Military History*, vol. 1 (Santa Barbara, CA: ABC-CLIO, 2009).

JUNE 7

On June 7, 1949, Governor Fuller Warren signed a law that ended free-range cattle grazing in Florida. For many years, free-range herds were the norm throughout the state. By the 1940s, the open range became largely the domain of poorer herders who had little or no grazing land for their cattle and hogs and allowed their animals to graze on unclaimed and public lands. By the late 1940s, the centuries-old practice was running into problems; livestock wandered onto claimed lands, often causing property damage to valuable citrus groves that had taken over much of the old scrubland, or they caused car collisions when they ventured onto highways.

FOR FURTHER READING: John Solomon Otto, "Cattle-Grazing in the Southeastern United States, 1670–1949: An Economic and Social Adaptation," in *Animals in Human Histories: The Mirror of Nature and Culture* (Suffolk, England: Boydell and Brewer, 2002), 56–82.

JUNE 8

On June 8, 2006, the Miami Heat basketball team lost the first game of the National Basketball Association finals against the Dallas Mavericks in Texas. The Miami Heat, featuring future Hall of Famer players Gary Payton, Shaquille O'Neal, and Alonzo Mourning as well as Dwyane Wade, also lost the second game but won the next four in a row to secure the NBA championship. They became the third team to win the championship after losing the first two games of the series. The win was the Heat's first NBA championship. They would go on to win again in 2012 and 2013.

FOR FURTHER READING: Marty Gitlin, *Miami Heat* (North Mankato, MN: ABDO, 2012).

JUNE 9

On June 9, 1699, Luis Rodrigo's party of Spanish and Native soldiers finished their expedition to Tampa Bay in search of English settlements. Rodrigo's group, composed of three Spanish soldiers, twelve Indian chiefs, and an unknown number of warriors, had been sent by the governor of Florida to determine the veracity of rumors that the English were trying to colonize Florida. Working with Native interpreters, the Spanish questioned local Indians who told them the English had been there but did not disembark from their ships. The English, they explained, eventually sailed away.

FOR FURTHER READING: Ronald Wayne Childers, "Historic Notes and Documents: A Late Seventeenth-Century Journey to Tampa Bay," *Florida Historical Quarterly* 80, no. 4 (2002): 504–522.

June 10

On June 10, 1990, the Miami rap group 2 Live Crew was arrested on charges of indecency after performing tracks from their new album, *As Nasty as They Want to Be*, at a nightclub in Broward County. The group was acquitted on October 20, 1990, after receiving widespread support from free-speech activists around the world. Harvard Professor Henry Louis Gates Jr. testified at their trial in defense of the objectionable lyrics. *Nasty* was 2 Live Crew's most successful album, in part because of the controversy over its content and its parental advisory sticker. In 1990, concern over the lyrics resulted in obscenity arrests of several individuals who sold the album.

FOR FURTHER READING: Wayne Flynt, "Religion at the Polls: A Case Study of Twentieth Century Politics and Religion in Florida," *Florida Historical Quarterly* 74, no. 4 (1994): 469–483.

June 11

On June 11, 1964, Martin Luther King Jr. was arrested in St. Augustine on the steps of the Monson Motor Lodge restaurant. The arrest occurred the night after the passage of the Civil Rights Act of 1964, a development that could only occur when West Virginia Senator Robert C. Byrd's fourteen-hour filibuster collapsed. The act specifically prohibits discrimination on the basis of race, color, sex, religion, or national origin. The arrest defied the new protection. King came to St. Augustine on the urging of its leading civil rights activist, Dr. Robert Hayling. Local civil rights leaders hoped King could bring attention to the city's resistance to integration and the activity of the Ku Klux Klan and other white supremacists.

FOR FURTHER READING: Dan R. Warren, *If It Takes All Summer: Martin Luther King, the KKK, and States' Rights in St. Augustine, 1964* (Tuscaloosa: University of Alabama Press, 2008).

JUNE 12

On June 12, 2016, a gunman opened fire inside the Pulse Nightclub in Orlando. The perpetrator, a twenty-nine-year-old man named Omar Mateen, announced his allegiance to the Islamic State (ISIS). The club was a staple of Orlando's LGBTQ community. The act was classified by the FBI as a terrorist attack, the deadliest such attack since those of September 11, 2001. Mateen killed forty-nine people and severely injured fifty-three others during the three-hour stand-off. Most of the victims were Hispanic because the club was hosting a Latin night. The attack brought renewed attention to the fight for gun control. Further controversy swirled when gay and bisexual men were turned away from donating blood in the aftermath despite multiple calls for donors to come forward.

FOR FURTHER READING: Joseph Allen Ruanto-Ramirez, Harjant Gill, Lucas Bulgarelli, Aniqa Raihan, Brandi Perri, Sik Ying, Sonny Nordmarken, Graciela Trevisan, and Jey Saung, "Orlando: Observances," *Feminist Studies* 42, no. 2 (2016): 528–539.

JUNE 13

On June 13, 1935, the Brighton Seminole Indian Reservation was formed as a part of President Franklin D. Roosevelt's Indian Reorganization Act, often called the Indian New Deal. The act granted Native Americans sovereignty over their lands and recognized their right to self-government. The Brighton Reservation, which consists of approximately 36,000 acres, has its origins to the arrival of Muskogee-speaking Cow Creeks in the nineteenth century. Today the reservation has cattle operations that are among the largest in the nation.

FOR FURTHER READING: John K. Mahon and Brent R. Weisman, "Florida's Seminole and Miccosukee Peoples," in *The New History of Florida*, ed. Michael Gannon (Gainesville: University Press of Florida, 1996), 183–206.

JUNE 14

On June 14, 1513, Juan Ponce de León and his Spanish expedition left Florida for Puerto Rico after being attacked by a group of Calusa Indians. Ponce had traveled south along the Atlantic coast before heading around the tip of Florida into the Gulf. Near present-day Naples, the Spaniards were flagged down by a Native man who understood Spanish. He informed them that a Calusa chief wanted them to wait for his arrival. The Calusa recognized the threat the Spaniards posed to the region. Shortly after their arrival, a war party that filled twenty Calusa canoes attacked Ponce's men and chased them away.

FOR FURTHER READING: John E. Worth, *Discovering Florida: First-Contact Narratives from Spanish Expeditions along the Lower Gulf Coast* (Gainesville: University Press of Florida, 2014).

JUNE 15

On June 15, 1569, Fort San Antón de Carlos was abandoned by the Spanish less than three years after it was commissioned. The fort reflected the troubled relations between the Spanish and the Calusa and Tocobaga. Reprisal followed reprisal, eventually leading to an assassination attempt on the governor of the colony, Pedro Menéndez de Avilés, by the Calusa; in retaliation the Spanish executed many Indians. These mass executions led most of the surviving Calusa to leave the territory surrounding Fort San Antón de Carlos, and as a result the Spanish lost their regular slave labor force. The lack of labor, in turn, led the Spaniards to abandon the fort.

FOR FURTHER READING: John E. Worth, *Discovering Florida: First-Contact Narratives from Spanish Expeditions along the Lower Gulf Coast* (Gainesville: University Press of Florida, 2014).

JUNE 16

On June 16, 1844, authorities in Pensacola released Massachusetts-born abolitionist Jonathan Walker from prison. Walker tried to help eight enslaved men sail to freedom in the British West Indies. As they sailed through the Keys, the ship ran into trouble and was rescued by a community of so-called wreckers, mostly men who profited by salvaging and selling goods from the ships. The wreckers seized the ship and turned the enslaved Africans and Walker over to federal authorities in Key West. The fugitives were returned to bondage, while the arrested Walker faced trial. Because Florida was still a territory, Walker's case went to federal court. It convicted Walker, issued a fine, and ordered him to be pilloried and his hand to be branded with "SS" for "slave stealer." Abolitionists paid his fine, and the branded Walker used his notoriety to lecture for several years about the evils of slavery.

FOR FURTHER READING: Alvin F. Oickle, *Jonathan Walker: The Man with the Branded Hand* (Yardley, PA: Westholme, 2011).

JUNE 17

On June 17, 1844, Congress authorized a pension appropriation for Milly Francis, a Creek woman who gained popularity in the United States for interceding on behalf of the captured American soldier Duncan McKrimmon during the First Seminole War. The daughter of Creek leader Hillis Hadjo (Josiah Francis), Milly became wildly and falsely known as a princess and the Florida Pocahontas. Her act of saving McKrimmon connected her to ancient southeastern Indian norms of captive taking. Francis, like the majority of Seminoles, was forcibly removed from Florida and relocated to Indian Territory. Francis died without ever receiving her pension.

FOR FURTHER READING: J. Leitch Wright, *Creeks and Seminoles: The Destruction and Regeneration of the Muscogulge People* (Lincoln: University of Nebraska Press, 1986).

JUNE 18

On June 18, 1964, a swim-in took place in St. Augustine to confront the persistence of Jim Crow segregation in public facilities. The protest was led by Mamie Nell Ford, who initiated the protest by jumping into the Monson Motor Lodge segregated swimming pool. The motel's owner, James Brock, responded to Ford's protest by dumping what he claimed was muriatic acid into the pool. Martin Luther King Jr. had been recently arrested at the same motel for attempting to eat in the segregated restaurant after the Civil Rights Act passed Congress.

FOR FURTHER READING: Dan R. Warren, *If It Takes All Summer: Martin Luther King, the KKK, and States' Rights in St. Augustine, 1964* (Tuscaloosa: University of Alabama Press, 2008).

White resistance to integration of public swimming areas in St. Augustine.

JUNE 19

On June 19, 1712, St. Augustine Governor Francisco de Córcoles y Martinez nearly incited a mutiny when he attempted to arrest the city's second-in-command Sergeant Major Juan de Ayala y Escobar. Born in Cuba, Ayala frequently blurred the boundaries of military official and entrepreneur to his own financial benefit. His reselling of captured English provisions endeared him to many Floridians, as the royal supply rarely met the needs of the town. Córcoles attempted to assert his control of the city and arrest Ayala on June 19 for this illicit trade, but the garrison of troops refused to act. After a tense few minutes that saw Córcoles's guards and Ayala's troops nearly come to blows, the two men publicly forgave each other to prevent civil unrest. In 1716 Ayala became acting governor of Florida.

FOR FURTHER READING: William R. Gillaspie, "Sergeant Major Ayala y Escobar and the Threatened St. Augustine Mutiny," *Florida Historical Quarterly* 47, no. 2 (1968): 151–164.

JUNE 20

On June 20, 1862, Union officers in St. Augustine received orders to require all citizens within US-occupied areas be administered loyalty oaths. While it had been customary to demand that Southern white men take loyalty oaths when US troops reoccupied territory, the inclusion of women in the order was a new measure. The order resulted from a recognition that defiant Confederate women had taken advantage of their gender to avoid retribution for their verbal and sometimes physical protests against occupying forces. In St. Augustine, after US troops occupied the city, some white women spat on Union soldiers, sawed down flagpoles so white flags of surrender or US flags could not be flown, and fired volleys at enemy forces.

FOR FURTHER READING: Tracy J. Revels, *Grander in Her Daughters: Florida's Women during the Civil War.* Columbia: University of South Carolina Press, 2004.

JUNE 21

On June 21, 1950, the *Miami Herald* published plans for the city's Interama, a site originally known as the Inter-American Cultural and Trade Center. The project was conceived as a permanent international exposition of the Americas as well as Europe and Africa. It was to include cultural, educational, trade, and recreational activities. The idea of the Interama evolved over the next several decades, but by 1968 when the site of the failed project was divided up, only a single building was finished. The site is now part of Florida International University and for a time had been used as a landfill for toxic and infectious hospital waste. Today, FIU Biscayne campus and Oleta River State Park sit on the property.

FOR FURTHER READING: Robert Alexander Gonzalez, *Designing Pan-America: U.S. Architectural Visions for the Western Hemisphere* (Austin: University of Texas Press, 2011).

JUNE 22

On June 22, 1564, French explorer René Goulaine Laudonnière, a veteran of the failed Charlesfort settlement, established Fort Caroline along the banks of the St. Johns River. The fort was supposed to be a

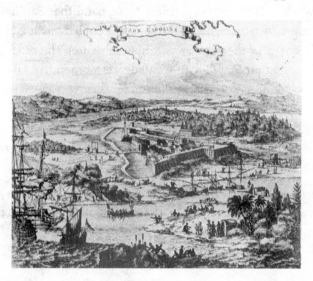

safe haven for Huguenots, French Protestants fleeing persecution in Catholic France. Fort Caroline also represented a new colonial territory for France as it sought to expand its overseas empire. Laudonnière brought with him approximately 200 colonists to settle in the area. Almost immediately after its founding, Fort Caroline faced a series of struggles. Its inhabitants suffered from hunger, and the Spanish and local Indians attacked the outpost.

FOR FURTHER READING: John T. McGrath, *The French in Early Florida: In the Eye of the Hurricane* (Gainesville: University Press of Florida, 2000).

JUNE 23

On June 23, 1549, Dominican priest Luis de Cáncer's expedition arrived in Tampa Bay to convert the local Native populations to Christianity. Cáncer, also known as Luis Cáncer de Barbastro, had some success in converting Indians in Hispaniola, Puerto Rico, and Guatemala. He could not match these successes in Florida. The Tocobaga living around Tampa Bay met Cáncer with extreme suspicion, even with a Native interpreter assisting him. Cáncer and several other missionaries were killed by the Tocobaga. Cáncer was clubbed to death on the beach while he prayed. Centuries after his death, the Vatican recognized the sacrifices made by Cáncer and other missioners and proposed that they be canonized as martyrs.

FOR FURTHER READING: John E. Worth, *Discovering Florida: First-Contact Narratives from Spanish Expeditions along the Lower Gulf Coast* (Gainesville: University Press of Florida, 2014).

JUNE 24

On June 24, 1699, Adjutant Luis Rodrigo's party of Spanish and Native soldiers returned to St. Augustine from one of the only documented seventeenth-century explorations of the interior of Florida. The Spanish gave detailed descriptions of the geography of Central Florida from Tampa Bay to modern-day Gainesville. The accounts describe the difficulties the group had penetrating the interior because of hard-to-locate roads and paths, and they describe the locations of different villages of the interior Indians. They note several rivers in the area as well as the flat land of the center of the peninsula. These descriptions were ultimately sent to the king of Spain by the governor of Florida.

FOR FURTHER READING: Ronald Wayne Childers, "Historic Notes and Documents: A Late Seventeenth-Century Journey to Tampa Bay," *Florida Historical Quarterly* 80, no. 4 (2002): 504–522.

JUNE 25

On June 25, 1868, Florida was readmitted to the Union after meeting the qualifications set forth by the federal government during Reconstruction. President Abraham Lincoln had begun the process by instituting the Ten Percent Plan, which allowed for a state to rejoin the Union when 10 percent of its 1860 voters had taken the oath of allegiance and pledged to follow the Emancipation Proclamation. After his assassination in 1865, Republicans in Congress pushed forward a much stricter policy. States had to rewrite their constitutions to include the abolition of slavery, the right of African American men to vote, equal protection for African American men under the law, and the inability to deny a man the right to vote based on "race, color, or previous condition of servitude." After Reconstruction ended in 1877, Florida, like the rest of the Southern states, began enacting Jim Crow laws that disenfranchised and segregated African Americans.

FOR FURTHER READING: Jerrell H. Shofner, *Nor Is It Over Yet: Florida in the Age of Reconstruction, 1863–1877* (Gainesville: University Press of Florida, 1974).

JUNE 26

On June 26, 1740, Fort Mosé, Gracia Real de Santa Teresa de Mosé, was stormed by the Spanish during the War of Jenkins' Ear. When the Spanish abandoned the fort, the British occupied it as part of a larger attempt to capture St. Augustine. The Spanish founded Fort Mosé as a refuge for African Americans fleeing enslavement in British colonies. The Spanish briefly abandoned the fort after several of its inhabitants were killed by British-allied Natives. When the British quickly occupied it, the Spanish and their Creek allies launched an offensive and retook the fort. During the battle, the British garrison was nearly wiped out and the fort was destroyed. Fort Mosé was the first free black fort and settlement in North America.

FOR FURTHER READING: Jane Landers, *Black Society in Spanish Florida* (Champaign: University of Illinois Press, 1999).

JUNE 27

On June 27, 1990, the *Miami Herald* published a column by Carl Hiaasen with the headline "In tourist haven, mayor sticks to guns." In this column, the satirist and best-selling novelist took aim at Miami Beach Mayor Alex Daoud because he registered four semi-automatic guns and a night scope as recent gifts from a company seeking a lucrative contract with the Miami Beach Police Department. Hiaasen pointed to the appearance of impropriety and connected Daoud with other public scandals involving guns and South Florida politicians. Local officials frequently complained about the bad press the area received because of Hiaasen's syndicated weekly columns and his novels. Hiaasen's books and articles often focused on the environmental consequences brought about by the rampant population growth and influx of tourists, all tinged with irony, sarcasm, a touch of bitterness, and more than a healthy pinch of satire and slapstick comedy.

FOR FURTHER READING: David M. Parker, "Is South Florida the New Southern California? Carl Hiaasen's Dystopian Paradise," *Florida Historical Quarterly* 90, no. 3 (2012): 306–323.

JUNE 28

On June 28, 1990, Alabama officials proposed that they and their counterparts in Florida and Georgia meet and figure out what to do with the ACF Basin, the watershed of the Apalachicola, Chattahoochee, and Flint Rivers. The basin has been the source of conflict between the three states because of Georgia's need for drinking water, Alabama's interests in it for navigation and recreational purposes, and Florida's desire to maintain freshwater levels in Apalachicola Bay to support its seafood industries. The three states have since met in court numerous times to address issues related to the ACF Basin. It remains an ongoing legal headache for the states, as they struggle to agree on any issue related to it.

FOR FURTHER READING: Jeffrey L. Jordan, "Conflict Comes to the Humid East: The Tri-State Water Wars," in *Interstate Water Allocation in Alabama, Florida, and Georgia: New Issues, New Methods, New Models*, ed. Jeffrey L. Jordan and Aaron T. Wolf (Gainesville: University of Florida Press, 2006), 20–29.

JUNE 29

On June 29, 1942, the HMS *Empire Mica*, a British liberty ship transporting gasoline to Britain, was torpedoed and sunk by a German U-boat in the Gulf of Mexico just south of Little St. George Island. The explosion could be seen in Apalachicola, where rescuers scrambled to find survivors. Only fourteen of the thirty-three crew members were pulled from the Gulf. German U-boats patrolled the waters of Florida throughout the war and sank fifty-six boats in the Gulf. The remains of the *Empire Mica* are now an underwater reef that can be visited by divers and fishermen. The 32,000-pound bronze propeller was salvaged by divers in 1981 and is displayed outside a restaurant in Panama City Beach.

FOR FURTHER READING: Kevin M. McCarthy, *Apalachicola Bay* (Lanham, MD: Rowman and Littlefield, 2015).

On June 30, 2011, the Dozier School for Boys at Marianna finally closed. Established in 1900 by the Florida legislature, the reform school was intended as an alternative for young offenders to the pervasive convict-lease system of the late 1800s. Juveniles sent to the school were supposed to be considered students, not inmates. The school quickly developed a reputation that countered its rehabilitative mission. The state closed the school after several law enforcement investigations uncovered years of systematic abuse and unreported deaths. The history of the school inspired Colson Whitehead's 2019 critically acclaimed work, *The Nickel Boys: A Novel.*

FOR FURTHER READING: Erin H. Kimmerle, Richard Estabrook, E. Christian Wells, and Antoinette Jackson, *Documentation of the Boot Hill Cemetery (8JA1860), at the Former Arthur G. Dozier School for Boys, Marianna, FL* (Tampa: University of South Florida, 2012).

July

JULY 1

On July 1, 1965, the Florida Legislative Investigation Committee, better known as the Johns Committee, finally disbanded. Named after its first chairman, Charley Johns, the committee spent nearly ten years conducting a wide-ranging investigation into supposedly subversive academic activities, civil rights groups, and suspected communist organizations as well as a crusade against homosexuals in state government and public education. Created during the paranoid atmosphere of the McCarthy era, the committee relentlessly harassed groups that were alien to the Pork Chop Gang legislators of conservative, rural North Florida. They published the so-called Purple Pamphlet about homosexuality that included so much graphic terminology and photographs of sexual activity that the committee was threatened with legal action.

FOR FURTHER READING: Judith Poucher, *State of Defiance: Challenging the Johns Committee's Assault on Civil Liberties* (Gainesville: University Press of Florida, 2014).

July 2

On July 2, 1951, the remains of Mary Reeser were discovered in her small apartment in St. Petersburg. Reeser's body was almost completely burned, leading media to call her "the cinder woman." Believers in the paranormal argued that her death resulted from spontaneous human combustion, with no other natural explanation. However, Reeser was last seen alive the previous night by her son, a physician, smoking a cigarette after taking sleeping pills. She likely passed away after the cigarette caught her clothing on fire rather than by a supernatural event. This explanation did not stop rumors from circulating about the supernatural for many years.

FOR FURTHER READING: Joe Nickell, *Real-Life X-Files: Investigating the Paranormal* (Lexington: University Press of Kentucky, 2001).

July 3

On July 3, 1968, the Florida legislature approved the revised state constitution. It was then sent for the voters' approval in November 1968. The revision was made to replace the 1885 state constitution, and proponents declared that a change was necessary to bring the state into modern times. The 1885 constitution undid many of the reforms mandated by the federal government during Reconstruction as preconditions for Florida's readmission to the United States. Since it was adopted in 1968, the state constitution has been amended more than 100 times; it established revision committees at regular intervals. The 1968 Florida Constitution also paved the way toward a more transparent government through its government in the sunshine laws.

FOR FURTHER READING: Mary E. Adkins, *Making Modern Florida: How the Spirit of Reform Shaped a New State Constitution* (Gainesville: University Press of Florida, 2016).

JULY 4

On July 4, 1868, civilian government of the state resumed after a period of military governance that followed the Civil War. This would be the first time African American men were eligible to vote in state elections, and many former Confederate men could vote for the first time since the war ended as well. The transition was fraught with violence and threats of violence. It also inspired renewed animus between Democrats and Republicans who had fought almost nonstop throughout the constitutional convention. Many white Democrats criticized the new governor, Republican Harrison Reed, as a carpetbagger who advocated a return to "negro rule."

FOR FURTHER READING: Allen Morris and Joan Perry Morris, eds., *The Florida Handbook, 2011–2012*, 33rd biennial edition (Tallahassee: Peninsular, 2011).

JULY 5

On July 5, 1890, the *Fort Myers Press* reported that local businessman and farmer Nelson Tillis returned to Fort Myers from Key West with a group of other travelers. Tillis was the first African American man to raise a family in the town. He was formerly enslaved by Willoughby Tillis in Fort Meade. After he obtained his freedom, he established a 100-acre farm in 1872 with his wife, a white woman named Ellen Summerall, and their eleven children. His son-in-law Wilson McCorpen had a nearby farm in Fort Myers as well as a stand where he sold ice cream and cold drinks that was frequented by an integrated clientele. Prior to the population boom that took place after the turn of the twentieth century, Fort Myers was relatively desegregated because of the services offered and provided by African Americans that were not otherwise offered by white residents.

FOR FURTHER READING: Jonathan Harrison, "The Rise of Jim Crow in Fort Myers, 1885–1930," *Florida Historical Quarterly* 94, no. 1 (2015): 40–67.

JULY 6

On July 6, 1961, Elvis Presley arrived in Florida to film *Follow That Dream*. Based on the popular novel *Pioneer, Go Home!* by Richard Powell, the movie followed the story about a family of squatters from New Jersey. The film was shot in and around Citrus, Levy, and Marion Counties. During the filming, one of the men working on it introduced his nephew, Tom Petty, to Presley. Petty, a Gainesville native, later recounted his encounter

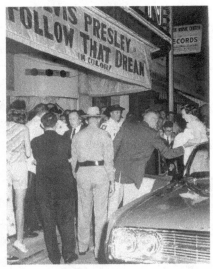

with Elvis and how he became an instant fan after the experience. Petty never became a cultural icon quite like Presley, but he sold more than 80 million records, making his one of the most successful musical careers in the twentieth century.

FOR FURTHER READING: Paul Zollo, *Conversations with Tom Petty* (London: Omnibus, 2012).

JULY 7

On July 7, 1983, more than 200 federal officers and police swarmed into Everglades City and arrested more than a dozen people charged with connections to a marijuana smuggling operation. They arrested sixteen more individuals in nearby communities. The crackdown, known as Operation Everglades, was followed by another sting operation in 1984 that saw several more arrests. The area around Everglades City was one of the most active drug ports in the country at the time. Fewer than ten years after the first Operation Everglades, more than 300 people from the area were arrested for marijuana smuggling. Everglades City had been a fishing village in the first half of the twentieth century, but fishing as a career path was shut off with the creation of Everglades National Park in 1947.

FOR FURTHER READING: Tim McBride and Ralph Berrier Jr., *Saltwater Cowboy: The Rise and Fall of a Marijuana Empire* (New York: Macmillan, 2015).

JULY 8

On July 8, 1942, a secret trial commenced for German spies and saboteurs who landed on Ponte Vedra Beach from a U-boat on the night of June 16–17. The spies planned to meet up with other German agents, dig up explosives they had buried on the beach, and blow up railroad lines and terminals, water and electric plants, and manufacturing plants. Instead, the plans were compromised by the mission's leader and his assistant, who turned over information to the FBI. All eight were found guilty, and six were executed on August 8. The other two collaborators were sentenced to lengthy prison terms.

FOR FURTHER READING: Michael J. Sulick, *Spying in America: Espionage from the Revolutionary War to the Dawn of the Cold War* (Baltimore, MD: Georgetown University Press, 2012).

JULY 9

On July 9, 1740, James Oglethorpe's unsuccessful siege of Spanish-controlled St. Augustine ended after nearly two months. The operation was part of the War of Jenkins' Ear. Oglethorpe, founder and governor of the British colony of Georgia, was tasked with raiding Spanish forts to the west of St. Augustine, including Fort Mosé, the first free black settlement in North America. Oglethorpe could never quite cut St. Augustine off from its supply lines; Spanish boats repeatedly outran the British ships, making the operation a total loss. Oglethorpe's forces were a mixed contingent of British regular soldiers, colonial militia troops, and allied Cherokee and Creek Indians. The war itself was a disaster for Britain, which suffered high casualties and lost some

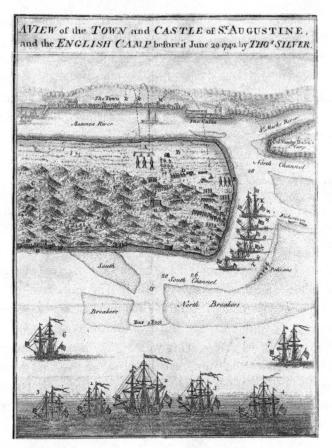

A VIEW of the TOWN and CASTLE of S.^T AUGUSTINE, and the ENGLISH CAMP before it June 20 1740. by THO.^S SILVER.

prestige. Though the fighting was largely over by 1742, the war was not concluded until 1748.

FOR FURTHER READING: Adrian Finucanem, *The Temptations of Trade: Britain, Spain, and the Struggle for Empire* (Philadelphia: University of Pennsylvania Press, 2016).

JULY 10

On July 10, 1972, the Democratic National Convention opened in Miami. Delegates nominated Governor George McGovern of South Dakota to be the party's presidential candidate. After the confused 1968 convention, the party overhauled its rules by opening the convention and platform to a wider audience. The eventual platform had planks such as abolishing the unpopular military draft, immediate withdrawal from Vietnam, guaranteed jobs for all Americans as well as a guaranteed family income above the poverty line, and amnesty for war resisters. The convention, which was influenced in part by the feminist and gay rights movements, reaffirmed its commitment to the Equal Rights Amendment. The Republican Party held its convention in Miami the following month.

FOR FURTHER READING: Hunter S. Thompson, *Fear and Loathing on the Campaign Trail '72* (New York: HarperPerennial, 2005).

JULY 11

On July 11, 1957, the Seminole Tribe of Florida's corporate charter was issued by the US Bureau of Indian Affairs. The process of getting the charter had been a grueling journey for the Seminoles. It began in 1953 when they were told their tribe was on the government's list for termination of tribal status. This would have meant the Seminoles would have been evicted from the lands on which they and their ancestors had lived for centuries. They received federal recognition later in 1957, and within a few decades the tribe went from impoverished to self-sufficient, taking a lead in the role for Native sovereignty.

FOR FURTHER READING: Mikaëla M. Adams, *Who Belongs? Race, Resources, and Tribal Citizenship in the Native South* (New York: Oxford University Press, 2016).

JULY 12

On July 12, 1826, the great-grandniece of George Washington, Catherine Willis Gray, married Napoleon Bonaparte's nephew, Prince Achille Murat. The wedding took place in Tallahassee. Prince Murat had been a Florida resident since 1824, when he bought property outside St. Augustine. Murat was president of Union Bank, a judge, and an attorney. Princess Catherine outlived her husband by twenty years, remaining at their plantation, Lipona, in Leon County. They had no children together. Their graves are located in the St. Johns Cemetery in Tallahassee.

FOR FURTHER READING: Doris Weatherford, *They Dared to Dream: Florida Women Who Shaped History* (Gainesville: University Press of Florida, 2015).

JULY 13

On July 13, 2013, a jury acquitted George Zimmerman for the 2012 murder of Trayvon Martin. Zimmerman was the neighborhood watch coordinator in his gated community where Martin was staying. Zimmerman pleaded not guilty to a charge of second-degree murder and manslaughter, claiming the shooting was in self-defense against an unarmed Martin. The jury's verdict angered many Americans and led to a new wave of black activism seeking racial equality. This movement merged with similar concerns over police brutality against African Americans.

FOR FURTHER READING: Devon Johnson, Patricia Y. Warren, and Amy Farrell, eds., *Deadly Injustice: Trayvon Martin, Race, and the Criminal Justice System* (New York: New York University Press, 2015).

July 14

On July 14, 1784, the new Spanish governor of Florida, Vicente Manuel de Zéspedes, was honored with a banquet by the departing British officials. Britain had recently ceded Florida back to Spain as part of the treaty that ended the American Revolution in 1783. The formal transfer of authority from Britain to Spain occurred on July 12, 1784. Years after Spain regained control, British subjects resided in the area around St. Augustine. During their shared meal, the British and Spanish officials feasted together and regaled each other with stories about the burdens of their jobs and otherwise overlooked their nations' rivalry.

FOR FURTHER READING: Edward J. Cashin, *The King's Ranger: Thomas Brown and the American Revolution on the Southern Frontier* (Athens: University of Georgia Press, 1989).

July 15

On July 15, 1999, the site of the *Industry*, a British sloop that had wrecked in 1764, was looted by persons unknown. In 1997, marine archaeologists discovered the *Industry*, the oldest shipwreck found in northeastern Florida. The *Industry* sank during Florida's first year of British rule. The *Industry* transported goods from New York to Florida, helping bring desperately needed supplies to the struggling colony. When it sank, the British struggled to salvage anything from the wreck. Modern looters were more successful. In 1999, archaeologists were stunned to find that thieves had stolen several of the sloop's cannons and perhaps additional artifacts that had not yet been described.

FOR FURTHER READING: Chuck Meide, "'Cast Away off the Bar': The Archaeological Investigation of British Period Shipwrecks in St. Augustine," *Florida Historical Quarterly* 93, no. 3 (2015): 354–386.

July 16

On July 16, 1969, all eyes were on Florida when the *Apollo 11* launched from Kennedy Space Center. Carrying Neil Armstrong, Buzz Aldrin,

and Michael Collins, the *Apollo 11* mission was the first to land people on the moon. Armstrong and Aldrin landed on the moon on July 20 and spent time exploring the lunar surface, while Collins remained in the spacecraft. NASA sent five more successful missions to the moon and averted near catastrophe with *Apollo 13* before scrapping the program after *Apollo 17*. The establishment of Kennedy Space Center transformed the east coast of Florida, bringing high-tech jobs to a formerly sparsely populated region.

FOR FURTHER READING: Courtney G. Brooks, James M. Grimwood, and Loyd S. Swenson Jr., *Chariots for Apollo: A History of Manned Lunar Spacecraft*, NASA History Series (Washington, DC: Scientific and Technical Information Branch, NASA, 1979).

JULY 17

On July 17, 1821, Andrew Jackson took formal possession of Florida after cession of the territory by Spain to the United States per the terms of the Adams-Onís Treaty of 1819. Jackson had been made governor of the territory by outgoing President James Monroe after having turned down the position several times before. Jackson's actions during the First Seminole War contributed in large part to Spain's decision to cede the land. During that conflict, Jackson repeatedly overstepped his authority and razed Seminole villages in the Panhandle. During his short stint as governor, Jackson and his wife, Rachel, lived in Pensacola, which they both hated because of its inhospitable weather and lack of social life.

FOR FURTHER READING: David S. Heidler and Jeanne T. Heidler, *Andrew Jackson: Myth, Manipulation, and the Making of Modern Politics* (New York: Basic, 2018).

JULY 18

On July 18, 1887, North Florida journalist Ellen A. Hill wrote in her column in the *Florida Dispatch* that there should be equality in marriage, especially when it came to finances. She declared that women were better suited to manage the household's money than men. Women, she explained, would not waste it on unnecessary expenditures such as tobacco and instead spend it on clothing for the children and other necessary domestic items. She also wrote various stories focused on women who successfully handled the financial affairs of their families, including the creation of a citrus orchard that eventually flourished.

FOR FURTHER READING: John T. Foster, Sarah Whitmer Foster, and Roscoe A. Turnquest, "A Liberated Journalist and Yankee Women on the Florida Frontier," *Florida Historical Quarterly* 91, no. 1 (2012): 33–48.

JULY 19

On July 19, 1949, a mob of white men rioted in Groveland in response to allegations that four African Americans, later known as the Groveland Four, had raped a seventeen-year-old white woman and assaulted her husband. The mob targeted Ernest Thomas, Samuel Shepherd, Walter Irvin, and Charles Greenlee. The mob burned down Shepherd's house and razed two others. The intention of the mob, in the words of its leader, was to "clean out every Negro section in south Lake County." They shot Thomas more than 400 times when he tried to escape. The other three were tried and found guilty. The court issued a death sentence to Shepherd and Irvin and a life sentence to Greenlee because he was a minor. Neither death penalty sentence was carried out. Lake County Sheriff Willis McCall shot Shepherd and Irvin in cold blood while transferring them for retrial. Shepherd died, and Irvin only survived by playing dead and waiting until he could leave undetected. All four were posthumously exonerated by the state of Florida's clemency board in 2017.

FOR FURTHER READING: Gilbert King, *The Devil in the Grove: Thurgood Marshall, the Groveland Boys, and the Dawn of a New America* (New York: HarperCollins, 2012).

JULY 20

On July 20, 1885, journalist T. Thomas Fortune's book *Black and White: Land, Labor, and Politics in the South* was published. Born in slavery in 1856 in Marianna, Florida, Fortune largely educated himself before attending Howard University. Fortune became a well-known journalist who edited several newspapers, including the *New York Age* and *Negro World*. Fortune also co-founded the National Afro-American League in 1890. Though it only lasted four years, it boasted among its members Booker T. Washington, W. E. B. Du Bois, and Ida B. Wells. It was one of the most prominent African American organizations at the time and a forerunner of the NAACP and other civil rights organizations.

FOR FURTHER READING: Shaun Alexander, *T. Thomas Fortune, the Afro-American Agitator* (Gainesville: University Press of Florida, 2008).

JULY 21

On July 21, 1948, Snooty the manatee was born at the Miami Aquarium and Tackle Company. He was one of the first and only manatees to be born in captivity. He was originally named Baby, but his name was changed when he got older. Because the state had only licensed Samuel Snouth to own a single manatee, Snouth transferred the young manatee to Bradenton's South Florida Museum, where he lived until his death in 2017, two days after his sixty-ninth birthday. Although he was the oldest recorded manatee, the museum reported that his death resulted from a preventable accident. He drowned after he swam into an area that was accidentally left open but did not have access to air.

FOR FURTHER READING: Thomas Peter Bennett, *The Legacy: South Florida Museum* (Lanham, MD: University Press of America, 2011).

On July 22, 1905, an article in the *Japanese-American Commercial Weekly* of New York City reported the founding of the Yamato colony in Wyman, near present-day Boca Raton. Yamato was a planned agricultural community for approximately twenty mostly unmarried Japanese men. New immigrants continued to arrive from Japan, but the colony never thrived. It struggled in part because of a blight that repeatedly struck its pineapple crops and because of racism against Asians in the United States. The last original inhabitant, George Sukeji Morikami, died in 1976. He donated his land to the state of Florida for a museum, now known as the Morikami Museum and Japanese Gardens.

FOR FURTHER READING: Ryusuke Kawai, *Yamato Colony: The Pioneers Who Brought Japan to Florida*, trans. John Gregersen and Reiko Nishioka (Gainesville: University Press of Florida, 2020).

Jo Sakai and Sada Sakai of Yamato, ca. 1910.

On July 23, 1839, a brutal raid on the Caloosahatchee River occurred during a truce that was forged between some Native Americans and General Alexander Macomb in South Florida. Approximately 150 Indians defeated a detachment of some 23 US soldiers at a trading post on the Caloosahatchee River. Only a few soldiers managed to get to boats and escape. Most white Floridians considered the attack a betrayal of a peace agreement that did not include the Native Americans who were involved in the attack. The raid led to a reopening of the war between the Seminoles and the United States that lasted until 1842. General Harney, who was publicly shamed by his defeat at Caloosahatchee, launched a brutal counteroffensive against Chakaika and other Indians deemed responsible for the attack.

FOR FURTHER READING: John K. Mahon, *History of the Second Seminole War, 1835–1842* (Gainesville: University Press of Florida, 2017).

JULY 24

On July 24, 1961, the *New York Times* reported on wade-ins being staged by African Americans in Fort Lauderdale. Throughout the South, cities maintained segregated beaches and left only small patches for African Americans. Broward County established a "colored" beach about a mile long on part of what is now John U. Lloyd Beach State Recreation

Civil rights demonstration at Fort Lauderdale's segregated public beach, 1961.

Area in Dania Beach. Access to the beach was difficult, as African Americans had to take a ferry from Port Everglades to get there. In protest, Africans Americans from Fort Lauderdale began a series of wade-ins on the whites-only beach. The city sued the NAACP and others in an effort to preserve segregation on the beach. Fort Lauderdale lost the suit and had to integrate the beaches.

FOR FURTHER READING: William G. Crawford Jr., "The Long Hard Fight for Equal Rights: A History of Broward County's Colored Beach and the Fort Lauderdale Beach 'Wade-ins' of the Summer of 1961," *Tequesta* 67 (2007): 19–51.

JULY 25

On July 25, 1955, George Went Hensley died from a snake bite, likely by an eastern diamondback rattlesnake, at a church service in Calhoun County. Born in Tennessee, Hensley led a Pentecostal sect that believed the Christian Bible instructed believers to handle poisonous snakes to prove their faith. Hensley, who reportedly had been previously bitten more than 400 times, refused medical treatment after the attacks. According to many accounts, Hensley's death did not change the beliefs of his parishioners. Though they witnessed Hensley suffer great agony from his fatal wound, attendees at the revival meeting indicated that they would continue the snake-handling tradition.

FOR FURTHER READING: Ralph W. Hood Jr. and W. Paul Williamson, *Them That Believe: The Power and Meaning of the Christian Serpent-Handling Tradition* (Berkeley: University of California Press, 2008).

JULY 26

On July 26, 1856, a Pensacola journalist rejoiced in a newspaper article at the news that a British ship returned an escaped slave who had stowed aboard the boat. The ship had sailed nearly 200 miles from the Florida coast on its way to Barcelona before the enslave man was discovered. Despite the distance from port, the captain returned the boat to Pensacola. The journalist admired the captain's adherence to the federal Fugitive Slave Act and declared that other ship captains should follow his lead. Prior to the Civil War, enslaved people repeatedly used ships in ports along the Gulf as means to obtain freedom.

FOR FURTHER READING: Matthew J. Clavin, "An 'Underground Railway' to Pensacola and the Impending Crisis over Slavery," *Florida Historical Quarterly* 92, no. 4 (2014): 685–713.

JULY 27

On July 27, 1816, a combined force of US troops and Creek allies attacked and destroyed the "Negro Fort" on the Apalachicola River. The fort, constructed and supplied by the British during the War of 1812, attracted hundreds of African Americans who sought freedom in Spanish Florida. They allied themselves with Native Americans wanting to distance themselves from the encroaching United States. Free, armed African Americans struck fear into the minds of Southerners, and the US military crossed international boundaries to attack the fort. The fort exploded when a hot shot hit the powder room. Many of the survivors of the explosion fled into the Florida interior, while many others were enslaved.

FOR FURTHER READING: Nathaniel Millet, *The Maroons of Prospect Bluff and Their Quest for Freedom in the Atlantic World* (Gainesville: University Press of Florida, 2013).

JULY 28

On July 28, 1937, Jane Cornell of the Association of Southern Women for the Prevention of Lynching appealed to the governor to prevent further lynchings in Leon County as well as the rest of the state. A crisis began when two African Americans teenagers, Richard Ponder and Ernest Hawkins, were killed in Tallahassee. Ponder and Hawkins had an altercation with local police that ended with a white officer being injured. The teenagers were taken from the Leon County jail by four masked vigilantes, who proceeded to administer extrajudicial justice. They shot Ponder and Hawkins nearly two dozen times. Messages condemning the killings reached the governor from as far away as New York and Chicago.

FOR FURTHER READING: Walter T. Howard, "Vigilante Justice and National Reaction: The 1937 Tallahassee Double Lynching," *Florida Historical Quarterly* 67, no. 1 (1988): 32–51.

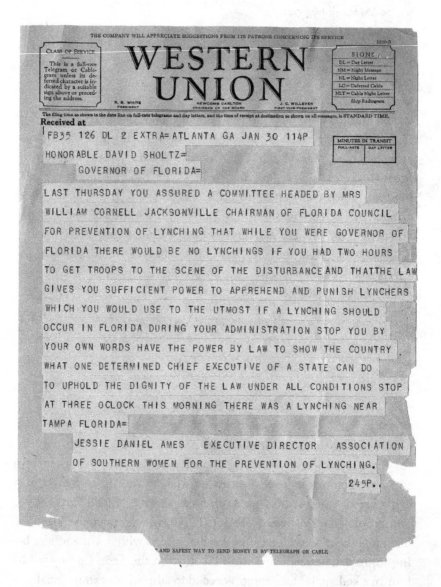

THE COMPANY WILL APPRECIATE SUGGESTIONS FROM ITS PATRONS CONCERNING ITS SERVICE

1220-B

WESTERN UNION

R. B. WHITE
PRESIDENT

NEWCOMB CARLTON
CHAIRMAN OF THE BOARD

J. C. WILLEVER
FIRST VICE-PRESIDENT

CLASS OF SERVICE
This is a full-rate Telegram or Cablegram unless its deferred character is indicated by a suitable sign above or preceding the address.

SIGNS
DL = Day Letter
NM = Night Message
NL = Night Letter
LC = Deferred Cable
NLT = Cable Night Letter
Ship Radiogram

The filing time as shown in the date line on full-rate telegrams and day letters, and the time of receipt at destination as shown on all messages, is STANDARD TIME.

Received at

FB35 126 DL 2 EXTRA= ATLANTA GA JAN 30 114P

MINUTES IN TRANSIT	
FULL-RATE	DAY LETTER

HONORABLE DAVID SHOLTZ=

GOVERNOR OF FLORIDA=

LAST THURSDAY YOU ASSURED A COMMITTEE HEADED BY MRS
WILLIAM CORNELL JACKSONVILLE CHAIRMAN OF FLORIDA COUNCIL
FOR PREVENTION OF LYNCHING THAT WHILE YOU WERE GOVERNOR OF
FLORIDA THERE WOULD BE NO LYNCHINGS IF YOU HAD TWO HOURS
TO GET TROOPS TO THE SCENE OF THE DISTURBANCE AND THAT THE LAW
GIVES YOU SUFFICIENT POWER TO APPREHEND AND PUNISH LYNCHERS
WHICH YOU WOULD USE TO THE UTMOST IF A LYNCHING SHOULD
OCCUR IN FLORIDA DURING YOUR ADMINISTRATION STOP YOU BY
YOUR OWN WORDS HAVE THE POWER BY LAW TO SHOW THE COUNTRY
WHAT ONE DETERMINED CHIEF EXECUTIVE OF A STATE CAN DO
TO UPHOLD THE DIGNITY OF THE LAW UNDER ALL CONDITIONS STOP
AT THREE OCLOCK THIS MORNING THERE WAS A LYNCHING NEAR
TAMPA FLORIDA=

JESSIE DANIEL AMES   EXECUTIVE DIRECTOR   ASSOCIATION
OF SOUTHERN WOMEN FOR THE PREVENTION OF LYNCHING.

245P.

AND SAFEST WAY TO SEND MONEY IS BY TELEGRAPH OR CABLE

July 29

On July 29, 1539, Spanish conquistador Hernando de Soto entered the deserted capital of the Ocale Province along present-day Silver Springs. The province, principal town, and chief all shared the same name, as was traditional for the Timucua. Once there, the Spaniards found some maize and other food to last them a few days but were soon forced to continue onward. Soto and his men also discovered Juan Ortiz, a Spanish explorer who had been captured by Indians while searching for Pánfilo de Narváez, who had disappeared during his own exploration of Florida. Ortiz would serve as an interpreter for much of Soto's expedition.

FOR FURTHER READING: Jerald T. Milanich and Charles Hudson, *Hernando de Soto and the Indians of Florida* (Gainesville: University Press of Florida, 1993).

July 30

On July 30, 1925, the district director of the Immigration Service in Jacksonville wrote to his supervisor about the rise in the smuggling of undocumented aliens on the new train lines to the area. The director expressed his fear that Florida would be overrun by nonwhite newcomers. The immigrants, he explained, utilized bootlegging networks that were created to circumvent Prohibition laws. Most of these immigrants were from Asia, in particular from China, and had been excluded by law from entering the United States since 1882. They were joined by immigrants from Russia and eastern European countries who were fleeing post–World War I Europe in search of a better life.

FOR FURTHER READING: Lisa Lindquist Dorr, "Bootlegging Aliens: Unsanctioned Immigration and the Underground Economy of Smuggling from Cuba during Prohibition," *Florida Historical Quarterly* 93, no. 1 (2014): 44–73.

On July 31, 1715, a hurricane sank a Spanish fleet of twelve treasure boats as it made its way to Spain from Havana. It carried large amounts of gold bullion and silver as well as chocolate, vanilla, cowhides, and other valuable goods. Eleven of the twelve ships sank off the coast of Vero Beach. It is estimated that as many as 1,500 sailors from the fleet of ships died in the wreck. A handful of survivors on lifeboats sailed to St. Augustine and alerted the Spanish to the situation. The Spanish sent salvage teams and salvaged what they could. Since 1715, six of the ships have been located. One of them, the *Urca de Lima*, is now part of Florida's Underwater Archaeological Preserve.

FOR FURTHER READING: Timothy R. Walton, *The Spanish Treasure Fleets* (Lanham, MD: Rowman and Littlefield, 2015).

August

AUGUST 1

On August 1, 1966, the body of Old Joe, an eleven-foot-long alligator well known to tour boat operators piloting glass-bottomed boats on the Wakulla River, was found dead at Wakulla Springs. Something of a mascot for the springs, the 650-pound alligator died from a single .22 caliber bullet between his eyes. In the 1980s, a local man claimed to have accidentally killed Old Joe while poaching smaller alligators. The preserved body of the large animal is on display at the Lodge at Wakulla Springs.

FOR FURTHER READING: Jerome Pohlen, *Oddball Florida: A Guide to Some Really Strange Places* (Chicago: Chicago Review, 2004).

AUGUST 2

On August 2, 1834, the *Portsmouth Herald* in New Hampshire published resident Dr. John Durkee's letters to his brother regarding the doctor's travels in East Florida. Durkee's letters contain his rich observations about Florida flora and fauna; he describes fish in the St. Johns River, the types of fruit trees that grew in the area, alligators on the river banks, and the contents inside several alligator specimens' stomachs. Readers were probably astonished by his being able to cook eggs in just twenty minutes by placing them in the sand and leaving them alone as well as by the unvaried diet of "hog and hominy" that he reported having three times daily with cane syrup.

FOR FURTHER READING: W. Stanley Hoole, ed., "East Florida in 1834: Letters of Dr. John Durkee," *Florida Historical Quarterly* 52, no. 3 (1974): 294–308.

AUGUST 3

On August 3, 1885, legislators finished writing the 1885 state constitution that repudiated Reconstruction. The so-called Redemption Constitution began to strip African Americans of the rights that are guaranteed in the Thirteenth, Fourteenth, and Fifteenth Amendments to the US Constitution that were ratified after the Civil War. The 1885 state document restricted African Americans' ability to vote by allowing the use of poll taxes, made school segregation mandatory, and disallowed interracial marriages. Like other southern states, Florida used the law to institute white supremacy when the US military withdrew from the region after Reconstruction. The 1885 Constitution remained in place until 1968.

FOR FURTHER READING: Talbot D'Alemberte, *The Florida State Constitution* (New York: Oxford University Press, 2017).

AUGUST 4

On August 4, 1842, the US Armed Occupation Act went into effect. The congressional act granted 160 acres of Florida land to any white man over eighteen, provided that he was able to improve the land, maintain residence for five years, and defend the land by bearing arms. All land grants under the act were at least two miles away from a military post. Given the exorbitant costs of the Second Seminole War, the federal government's objective was to inspire settlement by persons who would pay for their own defense. The Armed Occupation Act worked. The arrival of hundreds of armed white families transformed Florida, bringing what was once Indian country into American jurisdiction.

FOR FURTHER READING: Laurel Clark Shire, *The Threshold of Manifest Destiny: Gender and National Expansion in Florida* (Philadelphia: University of Pennsylvania Press, 2016).

AUGUST 5

On August 5, 1963, Clarence Earl Gideon had his second criminal trial in Bay County. Gideon appealed his first conviction for a break-in at a tavern because of a lack of legal representation. His case ultimately made its way to the Florida Supreme Court, which upheld the trial court verdict against him, and then to the US Supreme Court. After winning the Supreme Court case and with proper representation at his second trial, Gideon's attorney W. Fred Turner secured Gideon's acquittal after only one hour of jury deliberation. A best-selling book about Gideon's story was made into a made-for-TV movie in 1980 starring Henry Fonda as Gideon and José Ferrer as one of Gideon's lawyers.

FOR FURTHER READING: Anthony Lewis, *Gideon's Trumpet* (New York: Vintage, 1989).

AUGUST 6

On August 6, 2003, HB 1059 became law in Florida. The law was intended to breathe life into a pari-mutuel betting industry that struggled to compete with casinos on the Seminole reservations and the expansion of gaming elsewhere. The law allowed poker to be played at pari-mutuel facilities such as

jai alai frontons and racetracks. The act revised a number of provisions governing card rooms in an attempt to boost state tax revenues from pari-mutuel facilities that had been falling steadily since the early 1990s. These forms of gaming, which existed in Florida for decades, faced financial difficulties at the turn of the twenty-first century from increased competition by other types of legalized gambling in Florida and elsewhere.

FOR FURTHER READING: Jessica Cattelino, *High Stakes: Florida Seminole Gaming and Sovereignty* (Durham, NC: Duke University Press, 2008).

AUGUST 7

On August 7, 1840, Native Americans attacked Indian Key as part of the Second Seminole War. Most of the settlers there escaped, but Dr. Henry Perrine and twelve others died in the assault. The attacking Indians, widely known as "Spanish Indians," sacked Indian Key and burned all of its buildings. The survivors fled to nearby Tea Table Key, and the Spanish Indians followed them by canoe. There the residents of Indian Key attempted to repel the Native Americans by firing cannons that they had mounted on barges. The cannons' recoil, however, was too much for the barges to handle, and they sank. The Spanish Indians, likely descendants of the Calusa, were among the many Native American communities that the United States considered to be a part of the Seminoles during the nineteenth century.

FOR FURTHER READING: John K. Mahon, *History of the Second Seminole War, 1835–1842* (Gainesville: University Press of Florida, 2017).

AUGUST 8

On August 8, 1945, Virginia Key Beach in Miami was officially opened to African Americans. The beach was designated for African Americans in response to a wade-in at the segregated Baker's Haulover Beach State Park by dozens of African Americans to integrate the beach. Many leaders of the protest were World War II veterans who were frustrated by their inability to access Miami's famous beaches after proving

their patriotism overseas. Rather than desegregate beaches, local white officials opened Virginia Key Beach for the exclusive use of African Americans. Even though its waters were dangerous for swimmers and the beach was difficult to access, more than 4,000 African Americans used the beach within two weeks of its opening. It would become a site of African American recreation and activism.

FOR FURTHER READING: Gregory W. Bush, *White Sand, Black Beach: Civil Rights, Public Space, and Miami's Virginia Key* (Gainesville: University Press of Florida, 2016).

AUGUST 9

On August 9, 1916, the Florida Supreme Court declared that William Knott had won the state-wide Democratic primary for governor. Sidney Catts, a political newcomer, initially won the primary, to the dismay of party officials, who called for a recount. Catts would go on to accept the nomination of the Prohibition Party. Catts won the largest percentage of the vote in the 1916 governor election, making him the last  third-party candidate to serve as Florida governor. Catts rose to prominence by combining nativism with white supremacy and spreading a

conspiracy theory about Catholics arming African Americans to rise up in favor of Kaiser Wilhelm II. After one term as governor, Catts launched unsuccessful bids for the US Senate in 1920 and again for governor in 1924 and 1928.

FOR FURTHER READING: Wayne Flynt, "Sidney J. Catts: The Road to Power," *Florida Historical Quarterly* 49, no. 2 (1970): 107–128.

August 10

On August 10, 1977, Terry Bollea, better known to wrestling fans as Hulk Hogan, entered a professional wrestling ring publicly for the first time in Fort Myers. Born in Georgia, Hogan was raised in the Tampa Bay area after his family moved to Florida when he was about a year old. Throughout the 1980s and 1990s, Hogan was one of professional wrestling's biggest stars, winning championships in the World Wrestling Federation (now World Wrestling Entertainment) and World Championship Wrestling. Hogan's popularity extended beyond wrestling, as he appeared in dozens of movies and television shows and worked as a pitchman for various products.

FOR FURTHER READING: Hulk Hogan and Mark Dagostino, *My Life Outside the Ring* (New York: St. Martin's, 2009).

August 11

On August 11, 1955, Floridian Zora Neale Hurston criticized the *Brown v. Board* decision in a letter to the editor of the *Orlando Sentinel*. The prominent African American author found the ruling insulting because the US Supreme Court assumed African Americans wanted to associate with whites. Hurston insisted that she and other African Americans did not want integration. Instead, they wanted the courts to improve conditions at segregated schools and to insist that African American children attend school. In making this argument, Hurston gave voice to a belief that in some ways manifested that integration would destroy African American institutions rather than improve them. Hurston's most famous work is *Their Eyes Were Watching God*, a novel that revealed the vibrant community of the all-black town of Eatonville. Hurston died in obscurity at the age of sixty-nine in Fort Pierce. Today she is considered one of the most influential writers of the Harlem Renaissance.

FOR FURTHER READING: Valerie Boyd, *Wrapped in Rainbows: The Life of Zora Neale Hurston* (New York: Scribner, 2003).

AUGUST 12

On August 12, 2004, Tropical Storm Bonnie made landfall south of Apalachicola, beginning a particularly active and destructive 2004 Atlantic hurricane season. Twenty-two hours after Bonnie's landfall, category 4 Hurricane Charley hit Southwest Florida; some of the hardest-hit places were mobile home and RV parks in the heavily populated area of Port Charlotte, Punta Gorda, and Charlotte Harbor. Hurricane Frances struck in early September and was followed in quick succession by Hurricanes Ivan and Jeanne. The incredibly active 2004 Atlantic hurricane season caused more than 3,200 deaths and $61 billion of damage. The four major hurricanes of 2004 would be surpassed the next year with seven storms classified as category 3 or stronger.

FOR FURTHER READING: Jay Barnes, *Florida's Hurricane History* (Chapel Hill: University of North Carolina Press, 2012).

On August 13, 1620, the Creole religious scholar Francisco de Florencia was born in St. Augustine. He was the first Catholic priest who was born in the Americas. Florencia wrote *Historia de la Provincia de la Compañía de Jesús du Nuevo España*, published in 1694. It describes the first Spanish missions in La Florida, inhabitants of the area, and local flora and fauna. His writings offered a relatively optimistic view the region, in sharp contrast to his contemporaries' views. Most Spaniards in Florida focused on the region's lack of gold and silver and on the frequent revolts by its indigenous inhabitants.

FOR FURTHER READING: Jason Dyck, "La Florida in the Creole Imagination: The Frontier of New Spain in Francisco de Florencia's *Historia de la Provincia* (1694)," *Florida Historical Quarterly* 96, no. 3 (2018): 271–299.

AUGUST 14

On August 14, 1842, Colonel William Jenkins Worth announced an end to the Second Seminole War. He made the declaration after meeting with several Native leaders offering them each a rifle, money, and a year's rations of food if they went west to Indian Territory. Although many Seminoles reluctantly accepted the US government's offer, most planned to move to lands reserved for them in Southwest Florida. It is estimated that the war cost the United States $30–40 million at the time, about $960–970 million today. At least 1,400 US soldiers and

John Horse, an interpreter during the Second Seminole War, ca. 1842.

several thousand Seminoles died during the war. The total death count remains unknown.

FOR FURTHER READING: John K. Mahon, *History of the Second Seminole War, 1835–1842* (Gainesville: University Press of Florida, 2017).

AUGUST 15

On August 15, 1559, Spanish conquistador Tristán de Luna y Arellano founded the short-lived colony of Ochuse in what is now Pensacola. Luna was connected to powerful kinship networks, as he was a cousin of the viceroy of New Spain and of Hernán Cortés's wife. He was chosen to establish a settlement on the Gulf Coast and then blaze a trail to Santa Elena in modern-day South Carolina, where Spain planned to create another settlement. Luna's expedition, with more than 1,500 soldiers and settlers traveling on twelve ships, landed at Pensacola Bay. Disorder quickly followed. Luna was soon deposed by his men after he struggled to respond adequately to a disastrous hurricane that destroyed most of their already diminished supplies.

FOR FURTHER READING: Paul E. Hoffman, *A New Andalucia and a Way to the Orient: The American Southeast during the Sixteenth Century* (Baton Rouge: Louisiana State University Press, 1990).

August 16

On August 16, 1971, Judge William McRae ordered the end of any remaining de jure segregation in the Duval County school system. McRae, of the US District Court of Middle Florida, brought expedience to the US Supreme Court's *Brown v. Board of Education* ruling. Since that 1954 ruling, Florida and other states had dragged their feet in integrating public facilities. Some forms of resistance came through various lawsuits that attempted, in piecemeal fashion, to uphold segregation of facilities. McRae struck down those attempts.

FOR FURTHER READING: William Terrell Hodges, "Segregation/Integration in the Middle District of Florida," *Florida Historical Quarterly* 92, no. 2 (2013): 205–214.

August 17

On August 17, 1888, the *Tampa Journal* reported that Lizzie Carew would be customs inspector for the area. Her husband had held the position until his death on Christmas Eve. The decision to appoint Carew as her husband's replacement deviated from nineteenth-century norms. The customs inspector position was traditionally a reward for supporting a political candidate and a significant part of the spoils system that characterized the era's politics. Carew could not vote, as women in Florida did not gain that right until 1920 with the passage of the Nineteenth Amendment. She was personally appointed by President Grover Cleveland, indicating she was chosen because of her merit.

FOR FURTHER READING: Doris Weatherford, *They Dared to Dream: Florida Women Who Shaped History* (Gainesville: University Press of Florida, 2015).

August 18

On August 18, 1821, the first edition of the *Pensacola Floridian* weekly newspaper was published. Led by editor Cary Nicholas, the newspaper began one month after the transfer of Florida to the United States, making it the first to be published in the territory. Yearly subscriptions to the *Floridian* cost $5 in advance. Like most nineteenth-century newspapers, the *Floridian* published mostly advertisements and stories reprinted from other periodicals across the nation. Nicholas also published columns in both English and Spanish, as Florida had a sizeable Spanish-speaking population.

FOR FURTHER READING: Dennis Golladay, "A Second Chance: Cary Nicholas and Frontier Florida," *Florida Historical Quarterly* 64, no. 2 (1985): 129–147.

AUGUST 19

On August 19, 1970, "Walkin'" Lawton Chiles ended his 1,003-mile hike through Florida from Pensacola to Key West. The Democratic candidate for US Senate began his walk on March 17, meeting with local residents in every community he entered. His bid was successful, and he served as US senator from 1971 to 1989. After his Senate career was over, Chiles ran for and won the governor's seat in 1990. He held the office until he died of a heart attack in 1998. Chiles is remembered for his support of a school construction program as well as his lifelong advocacy for children and health care.

FOR FURTHER READING: John Dos Passos Coggin, *Walkin' Lawton* (Cocoa: Florida Historical Society Press, 2012).

On August 20, 1916, the *Miami Herald* reported on a temperance rally led by radical temperance advocate Carrie Nation during her visit to Miami. In her speech, Nation criticized local officials for allowing alcohol consumption to run rampant in the city. She claimed that officials were corrupt and proved her point by pulling out two bottles of whiskey she had illicitly purchased on a Sunday. When she left the rally she also harangued several men outside the tent for smoking and told them to go home to their wives. The news coverage of her visit to the city of "wickedness" revealed a cultural split in the young city, as some Miamians supported her crusade while others denigrated her message and methods.

FOR FURTHER READING: Paul S. George, "A Cyclone Hits Miami: Carrie Nation's Visit to 'The Wicked City,'" *Florida Historical Quarterly* 58, no. 2 (1979): 150–159.

AUGUST 21

On August 21, 1846, Anna Madgigine Jai petitioned to have her husband's will enforced. A prominent slave owner with land holdings in northeastern Florida and throughout the Atlantic world, Zephaniah Kingsley married his former slave Anna, and together they had four children. Anna was born in western Africa in modern Senegal.

Kitchen and main house, Kingsley Plantation State Park.

Zephaniah had legally manumitted Anna and their children in Florida, and the family relocated to Haiti after Florida became a US territory. Anna's white in-laws challenged the will, which left most of the estate to her and her children. Zephaniah died in 1843, and it took until 1847 for Anna to receive her inheritance.

FOR FURTHER READING: Daniel L. Schafer, *Zephaniah Kingsley Jr. and the Atlantic World: Slave Trader, Plantation Owner, Emancipator* (Gainesville: University Press of Florida, 2013).

AUGUST 22

On August 22, 1925, one of Lee County's new housing subdivisions included in its covenant that housing lots could be sold to white owners only. The restrictive covenant in the Tamiami Courts subdivision mirrored those used by many other subdivisions throughout Florida at the time. The covenants privately controlled who could purchase a specific property, ensuring that "whites only" neighborhoods would persist deep into the twentieth century. These Jim Crow restrictions operated alongside other state-sponsored forms of segregation.

FOR FURTHER READING: Jonathan Harrison, "The Rise of Jim Crow in Fort Myers, 1885–1930," *Florida Historical Quarterly* 94, no. 1 (2015): 40–67.

AUGUST 23

On August 23, 1891, the New York *Sun*, in an article entitled "A Florida Lake Gone," announced the death of Alachua Lake. The area, the lakebed of which is now known as Paynes Prairie, had been settled in the seventeenth century by the Spanish. It quickly became the center of the colony's cattle industry. The basin of the lake from time to time filled with enough water to allow steamships to cross it. In extremely heavy rains, Alachua Lake still returns briefly, as it did after Hurricane Irma in 2017. Today, this is the exception to the rule.

FOR FURTHER READING: Dave Nelson, "'Improving' Paradise: The Civilian Conservation Corps and Environmental Change in Florida," in *Paradise Lost? The Environmental History of Florida*, ed. Jack E. Davis and Raymond Arsenault (Gainesville: University Press of Florida, 2005), 92–112.

AUGUST 24

On August 24, 1992, Hurricane Andrew hit South Florida as the most destructive hurricane in Florida history at the time. Andrew was a category 5 storm with sustained wind speeds of at least 165 miles per hour. It killed sixty-five people and caused more than $27 billion in damages. One of the most lasting effects of Hurricane Andrew was the destruction of a facility that housed Burmese pythons, allowing them to escape into the Everglades. The similarity between their native habitat in Southeast Asia and the Everglades allowed the population to explode, which in turn caused many native species to become threatened or endangered in the area as they became prey for the voracious pythons.

FOR FURTHER READING: Jay Barnes, *Florida's Hurricane History* (Chapel Hill: University of North Carolina Press, 2012).

AUGUST 25

On August 25, 1710, the exiles and remnants of Apalachee people celebrated the feast day of San Luis, the patron saint of Mission San Luis de Apalachee. The observance of this feast day took place not in Florida, the ancestral homeland of the Apalachee and the location of the mission. Instead, it took place among the French in Louisiana. After the Florida missions had been destroyed by repeated Creek and English raids, the Apalachee evacuated and resettled elsewhere. The Apalachee are perhaps the only remnant community of ancient Florida to have maintained their community through the warfare, slave raids, and disease during colonization.

FOR FURTHER READING: John H. Hann, *Apalachee: The Land between the Rivers* (Gainesville: University Press of Florida, 1988).

Entrance to the reconstructed council house at the San Luis Mission historic site.

On August 26, 1990, the bodies of the first three murder victims in Gainesville of serial killer Danny Rolling were discovered. The murders terrified residents of the college town and their families across the state. Rolling would kill five college students in four days in the Gainesville area, mutilating the corpses afterward and posing them gruesomely. After he was caught by police and put on trial for the murders, Gainesville police were contacted by detectives in Shreveport, Louisiana, about an unsolved triple murder in 1989 that bore striking similarities to the ones in Florida. Rolling received the death penalty for the Florida murders, and he was executed by the state in October 2006.

FOR FURTHER READING: Mary S. Ryzuk, *Gainesville Ripper* (New York: St. Martin's, 1995).

AUGUST 27

On August 27, 1964, Hurricane Cleo struck Miami as a category 2 storm. It went back out to sea the following day. The storm developed around August 15 off the western African coast and hit Guadeloupe, Haiti, and Cuba before reaching Florida. Cleo was the third named storm of the 1964 Atlantic hurricane season but the first major hurricane of the year. It caused 156 deaths and more than $180 million damage. Most of the damage took place around Miami, where power

was out for several days, and the majority of the fatalities occurred in Haiti. Only two people died in the United States. Cleo was the first hurricane to hit Florida since Hurricane King in 1950.

FOR FURTHER READING: Jay Barnes, *Florida's Hurricane History* (Chapel Hill: University of North Carolina Press, 2012).

AUGUST 28

On August 28, 1565, French explorer Jean Ribault returned to the banks of the St. Johns River. He came with reinforcements for the undersupplied colony of Fort Caroline and relieved René Laudonnière. Ribault arrived just in time, as the colonists had run out of food and suffered in their frequent clashes with the local Timucua. Ribault brought with him 800 new colonists, but the French colony never became established. Spain had long since claimed all of Florida as its

The Promontory of Florida, at Which the French Touched, Theodor de Bry engraving, 1591.

possession, and it viewed the French as squatters and harborers of pirates who had attacked Spanish ships without provocation. The French colonization effort ended when the Spanish attacked and destroyed the French foothold in Florida.

FOR FURTHER READING: Jonathan DeCoster, "Entangled Borderlands: Europeans and Timucuans in Sixteenth-Century Florida," *Florida Historical Quarterly* 91, no. 3 (2013): 375–400.

AUGUST 29

On August 29, 1887, journalist Ellen Augusta Hill created controversy by challenging readers to respond to a *Florida Dispatch* column in which she declared that men enjoyed Florida more than women. Her challenge sparked a flurry of letters to the newspaper. Many white women wrote back that they actually liked living in Florida, pointing to the beautiful scenery or animal husbandry. Many women commented on some of the major complaints about Florida—the hot and humid weather and the prevalence of mosquitoes, snakes, and other pests. The women, mostly newcomers to the region, insisted that they had seen worse elsewhere.

FOR FURTHER READING: John T. Foster, Sarah Whitmer Foster, and Roscoe A. Turnquest, "A Liberated Journalist and Yankee Women on the Florida Frontier," *Florida Historical Quarterly* 91, no. 1 (2012): 33–48.

AUGUST 30

On August 30, 1602, Spanish officials led by Fernando Valdes came to St. Augustine to examine the feasibility and cost-effectiveness of keeping the settlement. Since its founding the town had been repeatedly attacked by Native Americans and English pirates as well as ravaged by hurricanes. By 1600 Spanish officials began wondering if St. Augustine was worth the effort to maintain. Florida itself was valuable to Spain as a stopping point for treasure fleets on their way to Spain from Mexico. After reading Valdes's report, King Philip III determined that St. Augustine was not paying for itself and ordered

the settlement dismantled. The English establishment of Jamestown in 1607 altered this assessment. Spanish royals ultimately decided to keep St. Augustine as a way of safeguarding Florida from other colonial encroachments.

FOR FURTHER READING: Susan Richbourg Parker, "St. Augustine in the 17th Century," *Florida Historical Quarterly* 92, no. 3 (2014): 554–576.

AUGUST 31

On August 31, 1985, the Walt Disney World Resort in Orlando closed because of Hurricane Elena. The storm, which had abruptly switched course from a predicted landfall east of New Orleans to northwest Florida, remained essentially stationary off the Florida coast. As it intensified, Disney officials closed the park. The first major hurricane of the season, Elena developed near Cuba from a tropical wave from the western coast of Africa and intensified in the Caribbean. Elena killed a total of nine people and caused approximately $1.3 billion of damage. Disney suffered comparatively little damage.

FOR FURTHER READING: Jay Barnes, *Florida's Hurricane History* (Chapel Hill: University of North Carolina Press, 2012).

September

SEPTEMBER 1

On September 1, 1927, US Treasury Department officials reported that thousands of undocumented immigrants had entered Florida. They did so by piggybacking onto the system that smugglers used to bring alcohol into Florida from Cuba. Traveling in high-speed and highly dangerous boats, immigrants from eastern Europe and elsewhere took advantage of Cuba's proximity to Florida and the relatively unpatrolled shores of the state. This route allowed them to bypass the immigration restrictions that Congress passed in 1921. American officials estimated that as many as 10,000 immigrants per year came to Florida's shores during Prohibition. Given the illicit nature of smuggling, there is no accurate way to measure those estimates. This path into the United States came to an end with the Great Depression and Prohibition's repeal.

FOR FURTHER READING: Lisa Lindquist Dorr, "Bootlegging Aliens: Unsanctioned Immigration and the Underground Economy of Smuggling from Cuba during Prohibition," *Florida Historical Quarterly* 93, no. 1 (2014): 44–73.

On September 2, 1935, the Labor Day Hurricane struck the Florida Keys. It was the first category 5 storm to be recorded in the United States. After hitting the Bahamas as a tropical storm, the Labor Day Hurricane rapidly grew in strength before hitting the upper Keys with wind speeds approximately 185 miles per hour. The storm continued along the western Florida coast until it made its second landfall near Cedar Key. The storm started making its way northward along the Gulf coast. The hurricane's damage was catastrophic. Few buildings between Marathon and Tavernier survived, and parts of the Florida East Coast Railway were destroyed. An estimated 420 people died during the storm, and Floridians suffered more than $100 million in damages, the equivalent of nearly $2 billion in 2019. It remains the most intense storm to ever hit the US at 892 millibars.

In the Ghastly Wake of the Hurricane

FOR FURTHER READING: Jay Barnes, *Florida's Hurricane History* (Chapel Hill: University of North Carolina Press, 2012).

SEPTEMBER 3

On September 3, 1783, the War of Independence came to a close when the newly independent United States and Britain, France, the Dutch Republic, and Spain signed the Treaty of Paris. As part of the treaty, Britain ceded Florida back to Spain, which had relinquished the territories two decades earlier. The 1783 treaty did not delineate a specific northern boundary with Georgia, leading to a territorial dispute between the United States and Spain that lasted for decades. Congress

would ratify the 1783 treaty a few months later, on January 14, 1784. The only part that remains in effect is Article 1, which recognizes the United States as a free, independent, and sovereign country.

FOR FURTHER READING: Andrew Stockley, *Britain and France at the Birth of America: The European Powers and the Peace Negotiations of 1782–1783* (Exeter, England: University of Exeter Press, 2001).

SEPTEMBER 4

On September 4, 1656, Governor of Florida Diego de Rebolledo dispatched soldiers from St. Augustine to put down the ongoing Timucuan revolt. Rebolledo instigated the revolt through his reactions to the British seizure of Jamaica in May. To defend St. Augustine from a presumed attack by the British, Rebolledo activated an Indian militia of 500 Timucua, Apalachee, and Guale men. At the same time, he ordered every Native American to carry seventy-five pounds of maize to St. Augustine to relieve a food shortage. His demands insulted Indigenous leaders, who protested to Franciscan missionaries that they should not have to share their resources when they did not have a sufficient surplus of their own and that chiefs should not be expected to perform arduous manual labor. When their demands remained unmet, the Timucua rebelled. Rebolledo ultimately put down the rebellion and had at least ten Timucua men executed.

FOR FURTHER READING: John E. Worth, *The Timucuan Chiefdoms of Spanish Florida: Resistance and Destruction*, 2 vols. (Gainesville: University Press of Florida, 1998).

SEPTEMBER 5

On September 5, 1836, the St. Joseph–Lake Wimico line was the first railroad to go into service in Florida. The line used a steam locomotive on an eight-mile stretch of land that was originally intended to be a canal. The following year, the company built an additional twenty-eight miles of track from St. Joseph to modern-day Wewahitchka on the Apalachicola River. The railroad was abandoned in 1842 when the town of St. Joseph collapsed after an outbreak of yellow fever. Today, part of the roadbed is used in State Route 71.

FOR FURTHER READING: Gregg M. Turner, *A Journey into Florida Railroad History* (Gainesville: University Press of Florida, 2008).

SEPTEMBER 6

On September 6, 1622, the *Nuestra Señora de Atocha* sank off the Florida Keys. The *Atocha* was heavily laden with silver, copper, gold, tobacco, and gems as part of a twenty-eight-ship treasure fleet leaving New Granada in Central America for Spain. During a storm, the *Atocha* lost the vast majority of her crew and her 265 passengers, with only five survivors, two of whom were slaves. The Spanish were unable to salvage much of the cargo because of a second hurricane the following month. In 1985, renowned treasure hunter Mel Fisher began salvaging gold, silver, and emeralds from the wreckage that he fought the state of Florida for the rights to keep. The Florida Supreme Court ruled in 1992 in Fisher's favor.

FOR FURTHER READING: Jedwin Smith, *Fatal Treasure: Greed and Death, Emeralds and Gold, and the Obsessive Search for the Legendary Ghost Galleon* Atocha (Hoboken, NJ: Wiley, 2003).

Mel Fisher viewing item retrieved from the *Atocha* ship wreck.

SEPTEMBER 7

On September 7, 1900, Giuseppe Zangara was born. Hailing from Calabria, Italy, Zangara gained worldwide notoriety when he attempted to assassinate president-elect Franklin Delano Roosevelt on February 15, 1933, in Miami. A construction laborer and anarchist, Zangara missed Roosevelt with his handgun shots. Several bystanders were hit, including Chicago Mayor Anton Cermak, who died from his wounds on March 6. Zangara was executed by electrocution at Raiford State Prison on March 20, only two weeks after Cermak's death.

FOR FURTHER READING: Blaise Picchi, *The Five Weeks of Giuseppe Zangara: The Man Who Would Assassinate FDR* (Chicago: Academy Chicago, 1998).

SEPTEMBER 8

On September 8, 1565, St. Augustine was founded by Spaniard Pedro Menéndez de Avilés. An admiral in the Spanish navy, Menéndez established the town to protect Spain's claim to Florida in the face of French and English competition. The town also served to protect the Spanish fleets that frequently hugged the Atlantic coast on their way from Havana to Spain. Menéndez received a monopoly on trade and

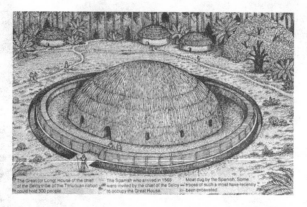

The Great [or Long] House of the chief of the Saloy tribe of the Timucuan nation could hold 300 people. The Spanish who arrived in 1565 were invited by the chief of the Saloy to occupy the Great House. Moat dug by the Spanish. Some traces of such a moat have recently been excavated.

permission to distribute lands throughout Florida. St. Augustine holds the distinction for being the oldest continuously occupied settlement of European origin in the continental United States.

FOR FURTHER READING: Michael V. Gannon, *The Cross in the Sand: The Early Catholic Church in Florida, 1513–1870* (Gainesville: University Press of Florida, 1965).

SEPTEMBER 9

On September 9, 1985, the *San Francisco Chronicle* published an article about how the popular new television show *Miami Vice* was changing the way people viewed the city. While Miami officials at first worried how a show devoted to crime-fighting would affect perceptions of Miami, they soon changed their tune when it became clear that tourists were lured by the show's images of sweeping ocean views and palm-tree vistas. *Miami Vice* also helped boost the flagging South Florida film industry and ushered in a second golden age of Florida-based films and television shows.

FOR FURTHER READING: Alison Meek, "Murders and Pastels in Miami: The Role of 'Miami Vice' in Bringing Back Tourists to Miami," *Florida Historical Quarterly* 90, no. 3 (2012): 286–305.

On September 10, 1935, the governor swore in the first eleven appointees to the new Florida Citrus Commission. The men were responsible for upholding the Citrus Codes, which included setting standards for shipping of fruit and controlling color-additive processes to make fruit rinds orange rather than green. The commission was especially tasked with advertising Florida citrus and marketing it to the rest of the country and beyond. The commission, which still exists today, both modernized and stabilized the state's citrus industry.

FOR FURTHER READING: Scott Hussey, "Freezes, Fights, and Fancy: The Formation of Agricultural Cooperatives in the Florida Citrus Industry," *Florida Historical Quarterly* 89, no. 1 (2010): 81–105.

SEPTEMBER 11

On September 11, 1964, Florida got its first taste of Beatlemania as the English rock band played at the Gator Bowl. The show was nearly canceled when the Beatles learned that the city of Jacksonville intended to segregate the audience. The band members changed their mind after they were promised that the city would allow an integrated concert. Even then, though, the concert was delayed when it was discovered that some unauthorized documentarians were attempting to illegally record the concert. Tickets for the concert were sold for $4–$5.

FOR FURTHER READING: "The Beatles Banned Segregated Audiences, Contract Shows," BBC News, September 18, 2011, https://www.bbc.com/news/entertainment-arts-14963752.

SEPTEMBER 12

On September 12, 1966, the *Gemini 11* rocket finally was launched from Kennedy Space Center. The flight sent astronauts Charles Conrad and Richard Gordon on a three-day mission into space. The mission was delayed because of a pinhole leak found fifty feet up the rocket. Technicians had to defuel the rocket before they could spot-weld their repairs. After the delay, the mission was a success.

FOR FURTHER READING: Kenneth Lipartito and Orville R. Butler, *A History of the Kennedy Space Center* (Gainesville: University Press of Florida, 2007).

SEPTEMBER 13

On September 13, 1951, President Harry Truman announced the creation of a pilotless bomber unit that would be headquartered at Patrick Air Force Base in Cocoa. This was one of several new or repurposed military installations in the state. The squadron officially formed on October 1, and despite the original announcement the special unit worked with surface-to-surface missiles rather than bombers. Florida took on a significant place in the military's training and testing during World War II. After the war, Florida kept its central place in this industry as it attracted various Cold War projects.

FOR FURTHER READING: John C. Fredriksen, *The United States Air Force: A Chronology* (Santa Barbara, CA: ABC-CLIO, 2011).

SEPTEMBER 14

On September 14, 1843, noted Florida planter Zephaniah Kingsley died in New York at the age of seventy-eight. Born in England, he lived in several European colonial areas in the Atlantic and Caribbean. Kingsley purchased a plantation in Spanish Florida in the early 1800s. Kingsley married one of his slaves, had sexual relations with others, emancipated several, and moved his mixed family to Haiti after Florida became a US territory. This more fluid connection between race and freedom typified the Spanish approach to slavery. Kingsley profited from the enslavement of Africans, even as his family straddled the lines between slave and free.

FOR FURTHER READING: Daniel L. Schafer, *Zephaniah Kingsley Jr. and the Atlantic World: Slave Trader, Plantation Owner, Emancipator* (Gainesville: University Press of Florida, 2013).

SEPTEMBER 15

On September 15, 1903, the first edition of the *Miami Evening Record* was published. The newspaper was renamed the *Miami Herald* in 1910 after Frank B. Shutts acquired it. Since its founding in 1903, the *Herald* became the newspaper of record for South Florida. During the 1920s, in the midst of a Florida land boom, the *Herald* was the largest newspaper in the world as measured by lines of advertisements. The paper nearly folded during the Great Depression but rebounded after being sold to a new owner.

FOR FURTHER READING: Nixon Smiley, *The Miami Herald Front Pages, 1903–1983* (New York: H. N. Abrams, 1983).

SEPTEMBER 16

On September 16, 1928, a major hurricane approached the Atlantic coast of Florida. It made landfall the next morning, and its massive storm surge flooded hundreds of acres south of Lake Okeechobee. More than 2,500 people are estimated to have drowned in the wake and aftermath of what has become known as the 1928 Okeechobee Hurricane. It was described in detail by Zora Neale Hurston in her novel *Their Eyes Were Watching God*. Hurston also provided an account of the effects of the storm on African Americans and other migrant farmworkers, who made up approximately three quarters of the fatalities. Some 674 people were buried in a mass grave.

FOR FURTHER READING: Robert Mykle, *Killer 'Cane: The Deadly Hurricane of 1928* (Lanham, MD: Taylor Trade, 2002).

SEPTEMBER 17

On September 17, 1798, Andrew Ellicott was forced to abandon his survey of the international boundary between Florida and the United States. Beginning in Natchez and working his way east on a joint American-Spanish effort, the surveying crew faced repeated challenges by Native American groups who saw the American and European survey as a breach of sovereignty and part of yet another land grab. Ellicott abandoned his plans midway. Rather than finish, he sailed with his expensive equipment and survey field notes from the Apalachicola River around the tip of Florida and back to St. Marys, Georgia. He never completed the survey.

FOR FURTHER READING: Farris W. Cadle, *Georgia Land Surveying History and Law* (Athens: University of Georgia Press, 1991).

SEPTEMBER 18

On September 18, 1926, a major hurricane struck Miami, shocking the city's residents, who had little warning of the impending storm. The hurricane, believed to have been a category 4, formed in the Atlantic Ocean only a week earlier. It killed at least 372 people in Florida; the exact total is unknown due to many migrant and transient laborers in the area only being listed as missing. The storm left more than 40,000 residents homeless and caused more than $100 million in damages. South Florida's tourist industry and economy did not recover until after World War II.

FOR FURTHER READING: Robert Mykle, *Killer 'Cane: The Deadly Hurricane of 1928* (Lanham, MD: Taylor Trade, 2002).

SEPTEMBER 19

On September 19, 1964, the family-friendly television show *Flipper* first aired on NBC. It was a spin-off of the 1963 *Flipper* movie about a Florida bottlenose dolphin, the pet of a boy who discovered and rescued it. The show was considered by many to be an "aquatic *Lassie*," as Flipper helps his human friends when they are endangered just as Lassie does for Timmy on that acclaimed television show. *Flipper* was filmed in part at the Miami Seaquarium; the familiar "dolphin"

sound Flipper made was produced by distorting the call of an Australian kookaburra. The series ran for three seasons. It came to an abrupt end when discussions at NBC about changing the show's format upset a producer who decided to cancel the show instead.

FOR FURTHER READING: Vincent LoBrutto, *TV in the USA: A History of Icons, Idols, and Ideas* (Santa Barbara, CA: ABC-CLIO, 2018).

SEPTEMBER 20

On September 20, 1565, the French Fort Caroline on the St. Johns River was sacked by the Spanish and most of its inhabitants were killed. After having traveled several days from St. Augustine to reach the French settlement, the 500 Spaniards led by Pedro Menéndez de Avilés attacked the French at dawn, taking them by surprise. Menéndez spared women and children, but the nearly 250 French men inside the fort faced brutal consequences. Some 200 of them are believed to

have been killed outright, with others being hanged later and the rest taken prisoner. Those who managed to escape the initial attack were later rounded up from the vicinity of the settlement and shot.

FOR FURTHER READING: John McGrath, *The French in Early Florida* (Gainesville: University Press of Florida, 2000).

SEPTEMBER 21

On September 21, 1959, the first day of classes began at the brand-new Brevard Engineering College in a former Methodist church in Melbourne. It enrolled 247 students, with more graduate students than undergraduates at the time. The college was formed with the mission of educating more students in the growing field of rocketry and space exploration. Its location was strategic along Florida's central east coast and proximity to Cape Canaveral, as most of the faculty had worked before on missile launches and rockets. The name of the school was changed in 1966 to Florida Institute of Technology.

FOR FURTHER READING: Gordon Patterson, "Countdown to College: Launching Florida Institute of Technology," *Florida Historical Quarterly* 77, no. 2 (1998): 163–180.

SEPTEMBER 22

On September 22, 1528, the explorer Cabeza de Vaca declared that the remnants of Pánfilo de Narváez's expedition left Florida for Mexico in rafts crudely made from their broken ships. The expedition had suffered terribly since it set out for Florida a year before. They were beset by a hurricane and several more storms in the Gulf of Mexico, where they lost much of their supplies and horses before landing near what is now Tampa. Narváez's group wandered northward, where they discovered the Wakulla and St. Marks Rivers. They decided to build rafts to reach Mexico; Narváez was lost at sea shortly afterward, while Cabeza de Vaca and three companions spent years trying to reach Mexico City, which they did in 1536. They were the only ones to survive out of more than 500 who left Spain with Narváez in 1527.

FOR FURTHER READING: David A. Howard, *Conquistador in Chains: Cabeza De Vaca and the Indians of the Americas* (Tuscaloosa: University of Alabama Press, 1997).

SEPTEMBER 23

On September 23, 1957, Governor LeRoy Collins delivered a speech to the Southern Governors Conference titled "Can a Southerner be Elected President?" Using Arkansas' firebrand Governor Orval Faubus and his bungling of school integration in Little Rock as a foil, Collins advocated a moderate approach to integration and the civil rights movement. Collins stated that the

commitment to segregation and intolerance cost southern states business and political opportunities, and he argued that only moderation on the issue could prevent Florida and other southern states from losing out economically.

FOR FURTHER READING: David R. Colburn, *From Yellow Dog Democrats to Red State Republicans: Florida and Its Politics since 1940* (Gainesville: University Press of Florida, 2013).

SEPTEMBER 24

On September 24, 1696, merchant Jonathan Dickinson and his shipmates found themselves washed ashore on Jupiter Island after their ship was wrecked during a storm the night before. Dickinson, a merchant from Jamaica, had been traveling north with his family and several slaves when they encountered bad weather and were shipwrecked on the southeast coast of Spanish Florida. They were taken captive by local Jobe Indians. Dickinson and his shipmates eventually made their way to St. Augustine, traveling more than 200 miles in makeshift boats and on foot. They finally arrived in Philadelphia in April 1697.

FOR FURTHER READING: Mary S. Mattfield, "Journey to the Wilderness: Two Travelers in Florida, 1696–1774," *Florida Historical Quarterly* 45, no. 4 (1967): 327–351.

SEPTEMBER 25

On September 25, 1764, British Royal Superintendent of Indians John Stuart wrote to the Creeks at Apalachee about King George III's desire to forge peace and friendship between English settlers and their indigenous neighbors. Stuart asked the Creeks to behave as "brothers" toward the English, who had just taken Florida from the Spanish after the Seven Years' War. In return, Stuart promised that the English would take care of them and ensure the integrity of the Indians' lands. Stuart had become familiar with the Cherokee after being taken prisoner during the Anglo-Cherokee War. He was, according to many accounts, one of the few Englishmen whom Native leaders trusted because of his consistent enforcement of their rights through treaties.

FOR FURTHER READING: J. Russell Snapp, *John Stuart and the Struggle for Empire on the Southern Frontier* (Baton Rouge: Louisiana State University Press, 1996).

SEPTEMBER 26

On September 26, 1958, the Miccosukee Seminoles sent a letter to President Dwight D. Eisenhower indicating that they wanted to settle an ongoing dispute they had with the state of Florida and the federal government over money and services they contended were owed to them by virtue of earlier treaties. The response was resoundingly negative, with Bureau of Indian Affairs Commissioner Glenn L. Emmons declaring that the Miccosukee were owned nothing. Emmons explained that the Miccosukee were considered part of the Seminole Tribe of Florida, and because they did not live on a reservation, the government did not need to provide them with services or funds.

FOR FURTHER READING: Mikaëla M. Adams, *Who Belongs? Race, Resources, and Tribal Citizenship in the Native South* (New York: Oxford University Press, 2016).

SEPTEMBER 27

On September 27, 1514, Juan Ponce de León received a royal contract from Spanish King Ferdinand II to further explore and colonize Florida and Bimini. The contract provided specific rules for the treatment of Indians following the Laws of Burgos, which were designed to justify ethically and religiously the forced extraction of Indian labor. Specifically, the Laws of Burgos put into place the system of *encomienda*, in which the Indians were taken from their lands and put on estates called *encomiendas*, where they worked for the Spanish. In return, they were supposed to be provided for by the owner of the estate (the *encomendero*) and taught the fundamentals of Christianity.

Gravure Anderson—Lamb Co.N.Y.

FOR FURTHER READING: John E. Worth, *Discovering Florida: First-Contact Narratives from Spanish Expeditions along the Lower Gulf Coast* (Gainesville: University Press of Florida, 2014).

SEPTEMBER 28

On September 28, 1953, Democratic Governor Daniel T. McCarty died at the age of forty-one. The Fort Pierce native suffered a heart attack shortly after taking office and never fully recovered. Before he was elected governor in 1952, McCarty was elected to the Florida House of Representatives in 1937 and served as speaker of the House in 1941. During his brief nine-month term, McCarty secured higher pay for teachers and scholarships for teacher training. He also opposed oil exploration in the Everglades. McCarty was the thirty-first governor of the state and the third of four governors to die in office.

FOR FURTHER READING: Allen Morris and Joan Perry Morris, eds., *The Florida Handbook, 2011–2012,* 33rd biennial edition (Tallahassee: Peninsular, 2011).

SEPTEMBER 29

On September 29, 1970, the Crystal River Archaeological State Park, under the name Crystal River Indian Mounds, was added to the US National Register of Historic Places. It was later made into a National Historic Landmark in 1990. The site contains six mounds, and archaeologists believe it to be one of the longest continually occupied sites in Florida. They estimate that humans have lived there for more than 1,600 years. Ancient Native peoples visited the site to bury their dead and engage in trade with other visitors to the area. It is because of these trade networks that artifacts from as far away as the Ohio River area have been found at the site.

FOR FURTHER READING: Jerald T. Milanich, *Famous Florida Sites: Mount Royal and Crystal River* (Gainesville: University Press of Florida, 1999).

SEPTEMBER 30

On September 30, 1889, the Florida superintendent of public instruction announced that the state would start hiring qualified African American teachers and staff to educate African American children. The announcement came prior to the US Supreme Court's landmark 1896 decision in *Plessy v. Ferguson,* a ruling that enshrined the doctrine of "separate but equal" into law. *Plessy* legalized segregation and so ushered in a host of public and private segregated facilities throughout the country.

FOR FURTHER READING: Peter A. Dumbuya, "Thomas De Saliere Tucker: Reconciling Industrial and Liberal Arts Education at Florida's Normal School for Colored Teachers, 1887–1901," *Florida Historical Quarterly* 89, no. 1 (2010): 26–50.

October

OCTOBER 1

On October 1, 1971, the Magic Kingdom at Walt Disney World in Orlando opened. The Walt Disney Corporation had been very secretive about what it called "the Florida Project" to prevent landowners from raising the prices of the large tracts in Central Florida the company was buying up under different corporate names. Also part of the Disney World plan was EPCOT, the Experimental Prototype Community of Tomorrow, which would not open until October 1, 1982. After Walt Disney's death in 1966 at the age of sixty-five, plans for EPCOT changed substantially from those Disney himself had envisioned. Following the Magic Kingdom and EPCOT were Disney's Hollywood Studios in 1989 and Animal Kingdom in 1998, along with several water parks and many on-site hotels and accommodations.

FOR FURTHER READING: Derek R. Everett, "The Mouse and the Statehouse: Intersections of Florida's Capitols and Walt Disney World," *Florida Historical Quarterly* 96, no. 1 (2017): 63–94.

On October 2, 1672, Governor of Florida Manuel de Cendoya held an official groundbreaking ceremony at what would become the Castillo de San Marcos in St. Augustine. The Spanish had decided that a stone fort was necessary for the protection of their settlements as well as to show France and England that Florida was already colonized. Both of those nations had attempted to move into Spanish-held Florida. The English tried to push out the Spanish from around Tampa Bay, while the French built a fort of their own just north of St. Augustine. A permanent stone fort, as opposed to a wooden-fenced palisade, was determined to be the best way to cement Spanish claims to the Florida territory.

FOR FURTHER READING: Jason B. Palmer, "Forgotten Sacrifice: Native American Involvement in the Construction of the Castillo de San Marcos," *Florida Historical Quarterly* 80, no. 4 (2002): 437–454.

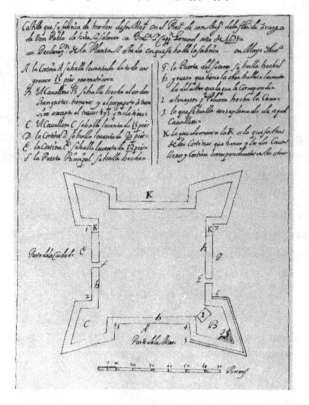

On October 3, 1887, the State Normal College for Colored Students in Tallahassee held its first classes. The idea for the college came out of the educational reforms after the Civil War. The State Normal College was designed to educate future African American teachers, a pressing need as segregation and Jim Crow laws began to flourish in the post-Reconstruction South. The college's name was changed to Florida Agricultural and Mechanical University in 1953. The new name indicated a change in the types of programs the school offered students. In 2006 FAMU was the largest historically black college or university in the country and remains the only historically black public college in Florida.

FOR FURTHER READING: Larry Eugene Rivers and Canter Brown Jr., "'A Monument to the Progress of the Race': The Intellectual and Political Origins of the Florida Agricultural and Mechanical University, 1865–1887," *Florida Historical Quarterly* 85, no. 1 (2006): 1–41.

October 4

On October 4, 1597, Florida Governor Gonzalo Méndez de Canço learned about the Guale rebellion. During the uprising also known as Juanillo's Rebellion, the Guale in modern northeastern Florida and southeastern Georgia rose up against the Spanish and killed or maimed the Catholic missionaries in their midst. Juanillo was a chief who asserted that the missionaries had hurt their communities by imposing various restrictions against many Indigenous traditions. The Christian missionaries forced the Guale to stop their practices of polygamy and divorce; they banned various dances and games and interfered in tribal diplomacy. To stop the rebellion, the Spanish destroyed the Guale villages and crops and ultimately forced the Natives to return to their ruined homes and fields.

FOR FURTHER READING: Paul E. Hoffman, *Florida's Frontiers* (Bloomington: Indiana University Press, 2002).

OCTOBER 5

On October 5, 1916, the author and folklorist Stetson Kennedy was born in Jacksonville. Kennedy worked in the Works Progress Administration, where, among many of its projects, he recorded stories, oral histories, and folklore throughout Florida. He served as Zora Neale Hurston's supervisor during her work for the WPA as a folklorist and writer. During his time with the WPA, Kennedy compiled the book *Palmetto Country*, with stories of cigar-factory workers, cracker cowboys, and sponge divers, among many other topics. He was an early proponent of oral history and recorded the tales he heard throughout his travels around Florida.

FOR FURTHER READING: Benjamin D. Brotemarkle, "Stetson Kennedy and the Florida Historical Society," *Florida Historical Quarterly* 90, no. 2 (2011): 265–272.

OCTOBER 6

On October 6, 2017, *The Florida Project*, a film about the dark side of Orlando's tourist industry, had its American theatrical release. The film depicts a six-year-old girl named Moonee who lives with her young mother at a rundown motel in the shadow of Disney World in Kissimmee. The pair try to put together some sort of life in the motel. Each has her own friends, while the mother faces intense pressure to feed and house her daughter every day. The squalor and hardship of these motel dwellers' lives is directly contrasted with the hordes of tourists visiting the resort to experience the magic of the Magic Kingdom.

FOR FURTHER READING: Carl Hiaasen, *Team Rodent: How Disney Devours the World* (New York: Ballantine, 1998).

OCTOBER 7

On October 7, 1763, Britain, by royal proclamation, established the boundaries of East and West Florida. The division of Florida, which was ruled by Spain as a single colony, was deemed necessary because of the distance between the two main settlements in St. Augustine and Pensacola and the danger of crossing the center of the territory. The division came as part of a decree that is better known for the Proclamation Line of 1763 that delineated all lands west of the Appalachian Mountains to be the territory of Native peoples. British officials hoped the division could keep Native Americans and English colonists separated so as to maintain peace between the two groups. It did not work. Instead, white settlers and speculators ignored the Proclamation Line and entered Native territories, thereby provoking conflicts.

FOR FURTHER READING: Colin G. Calloway, *The Scratch of a Pen: 1763 and the Transformation of North America* (New York: Oxford University Press, 2006).

OCTOBER 8

On October 8, 1885, cigar makers Vicente Martinez Ybor and Ignacio Haya began clearing land for Ybor City after striking a deal with the Tampa Board of Trade to obtain fifty to sixty acres of land. Ybor decided to move his cigar factory from Key West to Tampa because of persistent labor troubles on the island. His move did not solve the problem. In Tampa, cigar factories commonly faced conflicts between Cuban workers and Spanish office workers. Despite these conflicts, Ybor and Haya ultimately helped build Tampa into one of Florida's leading cities.

FOR FURTHER READING: Nancy A. Hewitt, *Southern Discomfort: Women's Activism in Tampa, Florida, 1880s–1920s* (Urbana: University of Illinois Press, 2001).

OCTOBER 9

On October 9, 1913, the secretary of the Navy appointed a board to select a site for naval aviation training. The board eventually settled on Pensacola, permanently transforming the future of the city. The Navy shipped sailors and other personnel as well as equipment to Pensacola and created what would later become known as the Pensacola Naval Air Station. At the beginning of America's entry into World War I, Pensacola had the nation's only air station. This distinction remained until

A few of the School Seaplanes and Hangars at U. S. N. Air Station.

1939, when the build-up for World War II dramatically increased the demand for trained aviators and crews.

FOR FURTHER READING: James R. McGovern, "Pensacola, Florida: A Military City in the New South," *Florida Historical Quarterly* 59, no. 1 (1980): 24–41.

OCTOBER 10

On October 10, 1765, John and William Bartram crossed the St. Johns River at Cowford, the site of modern Jacksonville. Naturalists and explorers, the father and son spent several months traveling through the new British colony observing and recording plants and wildlife. William Bartram briefly operated a plantation in Florida. He also made a second expedition through the southern colonies and spent an extensive amount of time in East Florida on the eve of the American Revolution. He visited several Native towns and became friends with Cowkeeper, an Alachua Indian who granted Bartram permission to explore his land. Cowkeeper called Bartram "Puc Puggy," which meant Flower Hunter.

FOR FURTHER READING: Daniel L. Schafer and William L. Schafer, *William Bartram and the Ghost Plantations of British East Florida* (Gainesville: University Press of Florida, 2010).

William Bartram drawing of two alligators in the St. Johns River, ca. 1773.

On October 11, 1935, the *Miami News* reported that a six-year-old Seminole boy dubbed "Little Osceola" was injured while wrestling an alligator to amuse his friends. Though Seminole men were familiar with hunting and trapping gators, "wrestling" them became a significant economic enterprise in the twentieth century as tourists flocked to see events that appeared to be authentic displays of Native American culture. During the matches, Seminole men performed in ways that thrilled audiences with their apparent dangers but used their knowledge of the animals to avoid getting seriously hurt. Reports of accidents were rare. Initially done for show and profit, alligator wrestling soon became a part of Seminole identity.

FOR FURTHER READING: Andrew K. Frank, "Grappling with Tradition: The Seminoles and the Commercialization of Alligator Wrestling," in *The Native American Identity in Sports: Creating and Preserving a Culture*, ed. Frank A. Salamone (Lanham, MD: Scarecrow, 2013), 131–141.

OCTOBER 12

On October 12, 1565, French colonizer and explorer Jean Ribault and fellow French Huguenots were killed in the Matanzas massacre. The crew had escaped the Spanish sacking of the French Fort Caroline a month earlier. Ribault and the survivors were shipwrecked by a hurricane that sank their fleet off Florida's east coast. They walked up the coast some fifteen miles until they encountered a Spanish patrol led by Florida Governor Pedro Menéndez de Avilés, who had led an assault on Fort Caroline. The Frenchmen surrendered in the hope that they would be treated better than if they resisted. That was the case for the prisoners who declared themselves to be Catholic. The rest were executed on Menéndez's orders.

FOR FURTHER READING: Matthew Jennings, *New Worlds of Violence: Cultures and Conquests in the Early American Southeast* (Knoxville: University of Tennessee Press, 2011).

OCTOBER 13

On October 13, 1947, the US Supreme Court began hearing the case *Sherrer v. Sherrer.* The case focused on a Massachusetts woman, Margaret E. Sherrer, who moved to Florida in order to divorce her husband, Edward C. Sherrer, so she could marry another man. She had followed the law by establishing residency for ninety days, filed for divorce, married the other man, and moved back to Massachusetts. Her former husband challenged the divorce in a Massachusetts court, claiming that she had not lived in Florida long enough to be divorced there. The ex-Mrs. Sherrer appealed. The US Supreme Court ultimately determined that the divorce was valid.

FOR FURTHER READING: Kristen Celello, *Making Marriage Work: A History of Marriage and Divorce in the Twentieth Century United States* (Chapel Hill: University of North Carolina Press, 2009).

OCTOBER 14

On October 14, 1997, the Florida Marlins secured the National League baseball pennant, punching their ticket to the World Series by defeating the Atlanta Braves in the National League Championship Series. The Marlins would go on to defeat Cleveland in a seven-game series to secure their first World Series win. It was an especially astonishing feat, considering that the 1997 season was only the Marlins' fifth as a Major League Baseball franchise. The Marlins added another World Series title in the 2003 season. The team changed its name to the Miami Marlins in 2011.

FOR FURTHER READING: Matt Doeden, *The World Series: Baseball's Biggest Stage* (Minneapolis, MN: Lerner, 2014).

October 15

On October 15, 1977, noted Florida rock band Lynyrd Skynyrd played a concert at the Hollywood Sportatorium in Hollywood, Florida. Unfortunately for southern rock fans, it was one of the final shows performed by the original line-up of the band. Five days later, as the band traveled to a show in Baton Rouge, the band's chartered plane ran out of fuel and crashed in rural Mississippi. Six of the twenty-six passengers died. The dead included founding members Ronnie Van Zant and Steve Gaines, backup singer Cassie Gaines, and Gaines's sister.

FOR FURTHER READING: Mark Ribowski, *Whiskey Bottles and Brand-New Cars: The Fast Life and Sudden Death of Lynyrd Skynyrd* (Chicago: Chicago Review, 2015).

October 16

On October 16, 1962, the Cuban missile crisis began. The diplomatic crisis, which lasted until October 28, was a confrontation between the United States and the Soviet Union over the deployment of nuclear missiles in Cuba. The discovery of the presence of missile facilities, just ninety miles from the coast of Florida, brought Cold War tensions to unprecedented heights. The United States responded with a naval blockade to prevent the Soviets from supplying more missiles to Cuba. Negotiations between the United States and USSR finally resulted in the removal of the missiles from Cuba and the secret removal of US missiles in Turkey. The crisis was the closest the two superpowers ever came to fighting a nuclear war.

FOR FURTHER READING: Robert F. Kennedy, *Thirteen Days: A Memoir of the Cuban Missile Crisis* (New York: Norton, 2011).

October 17

On October 17, 1933, Victor Licata was apprehended by police in his Tampa home. The twenty-one-year-old Licata murdered his parents, two brothers, and sister with an axe. After he was captured, police

claimed his use of marijuana made him crazy, even though Licata had a history of mental illness. The story contributed to the widespread notion that marijuana made people go into murderous fits and inspired the 1936 film *Reefer Madness*, also known as *Tell Your Children*, which was intended to warn parents about the dangers of the drug. Licata was never charged with murder. Instead, he was sent to the Florida State Hospital for the Insane, where he committed suicide in 1950.

FOR FURTHER READING: Larry Sloman, *Reefer Madness: The History of Marijuana in America* (Indianapolis, IN: Bobbs-Merrill, 1979).

OCTOBER 18

On October 18, 1817, 110 Africans were purchased on Amelia Island to be smuggled into the United States in violation of the slave importation ban of 1808. The Africans were on a Spanish ship bound for Cuba when pirates captured it and brought it to Florida. The illegally enslaved Africans were taken from Florida to Georgia through Native

American lands on behalf of US Indian agent David B. Mitchell, who was eventually fired without prosecution. This event shows Spanish Florida's contradictory nature for African-descended people, as the colony was long considered by some to be a place to seek freedom.

FOR FURTHER READING: Andrew K. Frank, "Slave Refuge and Gateway: David B. Mitchell on the Paradox of the Florida Frontier," in *Africa in Florida: Five Hundred Years of African Presence in the Sunshine State*, ed. Amanda Carlson and Robin Poynor (Gainesville: University Press of Florida, 2014), 137–149.

OCTOBER 19

On October 19, 1838, US Army surgeon Samuel Forry penned a letter to a friend describing events of the Second Seminole War. In this and subsequent letters, Forry described many of the medical miseries of the war. He also wrote about excavating an Indian mound west of Fort Taylor in Orange County. The doctor only located some "trinkets" and guessed that they were recently placed rather than of ancient origin. Among the items Forry told his friend he found at the mound were human bones, iron pieces nearly destroyed through oxidation, silver ornaments, beads, and "other Indian relics." Forry's amateur digging provides one of the earliest recorded examples of archaeology of Florida.

FOR FURTHER READING: Samuel Forry, "Letters of Samuel Forry, Surgeon U. S. Army, 1837–1838, Part III," *Florida Historical Society Quarterly* 7, no. 1 (1928): 88–105.

OCTOBER 20

On October 20, 1566, Spanish explorer and administrator Pedro Menéndez de Avilés wrote a letter to the Crown about the governance of La Florida as it related to the Indigenous communities in South Florida. He also discussed his friendship with Carlos, the chief of the Calusa Indians in southwestern Florida. In particular, he focused on how his friendship with Carlos allowed the Spanish to make peace with other

Native groups. Menéndez noted that he and Carlos hoped the Spanish could befriend all of the Indigenous peoples in Florida. Menéndez's vision of a pan-Indian alliance with the Spaniards did not come to fruition, as Native Americans repeatedly rejected Spanish rule and rebellions occurred throughout La Florida.

FOR FURTHER READING: John E. Worth, *Discovering Florida: First-Contact Narratives from Spanish Expeditions along the Lower Gulf Coast* (Gainesville: University Press of Florida, 2014).

OCTOBER 21

On October 21, 1837, the US military under Thomas Jesup's command captured Osceola and seventy-five other Seminole Indians who held a white flag of truce. The Native contingent had camped near St. Augustine to discuss a diplomatic end to the Second Seminole War with the United States. They flew a white flag made from the cloth that was distributed by the US military explicitly to signal an approach for diplomatic talks. Jesup knew that he was violating military protocol when he imprisoned the Seminoles in the false hope that his doing so would

bring the war to a close. Osceola died a few months later while imprisoned in South Carolina. The war lasted until 1842.

FOR FURTHER READING: John Missall and Mary Lou Missall, *The Seminole
Wars: America's Longest Indian Conflict* (Gainesville: University Press of
Florida, 2004).

OCTOBER 22

On October 22, 1957, the *New York Times* reported on the remarkable
growth around Orlando. The city was hardly the metropolis that followed the construction of Disney World a decade later, but the expansion of the Central Florida town seemed to emerge out of nothing.
Like many towns in Florida, the post–World War II growth of Florida
had much to do with the expansion in the aerospace and military-in-
dustrial sector. In 1957, housing and other construction permits soared
to nearly 70 percent more than in 1956. The arrival of Martin-Marietta
alone created more than 10,000 new jobs.

FOR FURTHER READING: Gary R. Mormino, *Land of Sunshine, State of
Dreams: A Social History of Modern Florida* (Gainesville: University Press of
Florida, 2005).

OCTOBER 23

On October 23, 1987, final preparations were made for the Wakulla
Springs expedition in North Florida. Under the leadership of Bill
Stone, an engineer and inventor, the twenty-member team mapped
more than 3,000 meters of underwater passages and chambers from
seven interlocking tunnels. The expedition took seventy days. Among
the technological advances made by this cave-diving unit were a por-
table underwater habitat to house up to six divers, the Cis-Lunar MK-1
rebreather (a computer-controlled life-support system), and a variety of
underwater scooters and sleds for gear transportation.

FOR FURTHER READING: Julie Hauserman, *Drawn to the Deep: The
Remarkable Underwater Explorations of Wes Skiles* (Gainesville: University
Press of Florida, 2018).

October 24

On October 24, 2005, Hurricane Wilma made landfall near Cape Romano. Wilma was one of the storms of the devastating 2005 Atlantic hurricane season, along with Hurricanes Katrina and Rita. At the time, these three storms were among the ten most intense Atlantic hurricanes ever recorded. After forming in the Caribbean, Wilma began moving westward and reached Mexico's Yucatán Peninsula. It then made a sharp turn east and headed directly to Florida. Its central pressure registered 882 millibars at one point, making it the second-most intense Atlantic hurricane recorded to date. More than eighty people were killed, and damages were estimated at more than $27 billion.

FOR FURTHER READING: Jay Barnes, *Florida's Hurricane History* (Chapel Hill: University of North Carolina Press, 2012).

Flooded street in Key West.

October 25

On October 25, 1885, writer Lafcadio Hearn published an account of his trip to Florida to find the mythical Fountain of Youth. The account, which appeared in the New Orleans *Times-Democrat*, played an important role in the spread of the myth. Hearn was an impressionist writer who, before his Florida vacation, had penned works about hurricanes and a travelogue of the French West Indies. In his story of searching

for the Fountain of Youth he described the "antiquated" nature of Florida in its lush, verdant glory. Since Hearn's account, hundreds of restaurants, housing developments, vacation spots, health spas, and other business enterprises have lured clients with Florida's undying attachment to the myth.

FOR FURTHER READING: Maxwell J. Stillwell, "By the Shores of the Phosphorescent Seas: Lafcadio Hearn's Journey to Florida's Mysterious Fountain," *Florida Historical Quarterly* 93, no. 4 (2015): 538–552.

OCTOBER 26

On October 26, 1934, Claude Neal, an African American agricultural worker, was lynched in Jackson County. Though little evidence connected him to any crimes, Neal was arrested on charges of rape and murder. He was moved to multiple jails in North Florida and eventually in Alabama for his protection. When a lynch mob learned of his location, authorities removed him from the jail in Brewton, Alabama, and took him back to Jackson County, Florida. The NAACP and others protested and fought to have him protected. Their efforts were to no avail. A mob seized him from the Jackson County jail, tortured, and then murdered him. The heinousness of the actions of the white lynch mob drew condemnation even in parts of the white South, which had tolerated if not endorsed earlier lynchings.

FOR FURTHER READING: Tameka Bradley Hobbs, *Democracy Abroad, Lynching at Home: Racial Violence in Florida* (Gainesville: University Press of Florida, 2016).

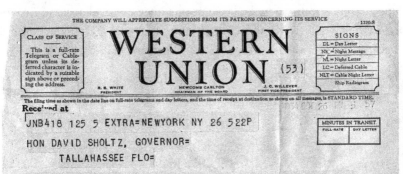

THE COMPANY WILL APPRECIATE SUGGESTIONS FROM ITS PATRONS CONCERNING ITS SERVICE

1220-S

WESTERN UNION (53)

CLASS OF SERVICE

This is a full-rate Telegram or Cablegram unless its deferred character is indicated by a suitable sign above or preceding the address.

R. B. WHITE PRESIDENT   NEWCOMB CARLTON CHAIRMAN OF THE BOARD   J. C. WILLEVER FIRST VICE-PRESIDENT

SIGNS

DL = Day Letter
NM = Night Message
NL = Night Letter
LC = Deferred Cable
NLT = Cable Night Letter
Ship Radiogram

The filing time as shown in the date line on full-rate telegrams and day letters, and the time of receipt at destination as shown on all messages, is STANDARD TIME.

Received at

JNB418 125 5 EXTRA=NEWYORK NY 26 522P

MINUTES IN TRANSIT
FULL-RATE   DAY LETTER

HON DAVID SHOLTZ, GOVERNOR=
      TALLAHASSEE FLO=

ASSOCIATED PRESS JUST INFORMED US THAT JOHN P HARRELL
SHERIFF OF WASHINGTON COUNTY HAS ANNOUNCED THAT TONIGHT
BETWEEN EIGHT AND NINE OCLOCK A MOB WILL TAKE CLAUDE NEALE
CHARGED WITH MURDER TIE HIM TO STAKE NEAR GREENWOOD AND
PERMIT FATHER OF DEAD GIRL TO LIGHT FIRE TO BURN NEALE TO
DEATH STOP EVERY DECENT PERSON NORTH AND SOUTH LOOKS TO YOU
TO TAKE EVERY POSSIBLE STEP TO AVOID THIS DISGRACE UPON THE
STATE OF FLORIDA STOP DOTHAN ALABAMA EAGLE ALSO ANNOUNCES THAT
NEGRO IS BEING HELD BY MOB FOUR MILES FROM SCENE WHERE HE
IS TO BE BURNED AT STAKE STOP WE URGE UPON YOU TO TAKE
IMMEDIATE STEPS TO RESCUE NEGRO FROM MOB AND PLACE HIM IN
SAFE CUSTODY=
      WALTER WHITE   SECRETARY   NATIONAL ASSOCIATION FOR
      THE ADVANCEMENT OF COLORED PEOPLE   SIXTY NINE FIFTH
      AVENUE.

OCTOBER 27

On October 27, 1810, President James Madison argued that the United States should take possession of the Republic of West Florida before it fell into "unfriendly hands." West Florida had proclaimed its independence from Spain earlier in the year and sought to be either incorporated into the United States or recognized as sovereign in its own right.

Madison, along with many other American expansionists, considered West Florida part of the Louisiana Territory that France had sold the US in 1803. Many of the citizens of the territory were American land speculators hoping to make large profits once the land became American. Shortly afterward, the United States annexed the territory, and it became the Florida parishes of modern eastern Louisiana.

FOR FURTHER READING: Samuel C. Hyde, "Introduction: Setting a Precedent for Regional Revolution: The West Florida Revolt Considered," *Florida Historical Quarterly* 90, no. 2 (2011): 121–132.

OCTOBER 28

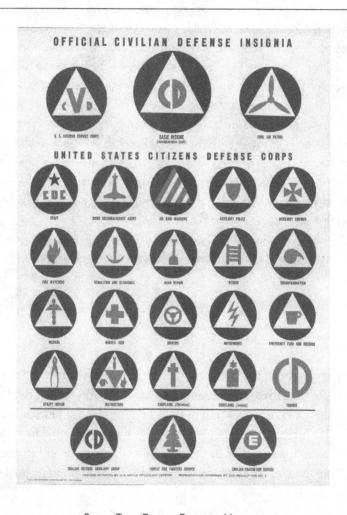

On October 28, 1942, an airplane flown by Albert Crabtree crashed into the Atlantic Ocean after the plane's engine died just off the coast of St. Augustine. Crabtree and his observer, Lieutenant Francis McLaughlin, were on a routine patrol looking for submarines during World War II. Neither man was injured in the crash. The two were rescued by the Coast Guard after two hours of floating in the ocean. Crabtree and McLaughlin were part of a civilian defense effort, the Civil Air Patrol. It patrolled the offshore waters of the United States as a way of alleviating manpower shortages the country faced periodically throughout the war.

FOR FURTHER READING: Thomas Reilly, "Florida's Flying Minute Men: The Civil Air Patrol, 1941–1943," *Florida Historical Quarterly* 76, no. 4 (1998): 417–438.

OCTOBER 29

On October 29, 2007, Jesse J. McCrary Jr. passed away. Hailing from Blitchton in Marion County, McCrary earned political science and law degrees from Florida A&M University in 1960 and 1965, respectively. McCrary served as an Army officer between his stints at FAMU. He earned notoriety for serving as lead counsel and winning the US Supreme Court case *Williams v. Florida* in 1970. In it, he became the first

African American to serve as legal representation for a southern state before the US Supreme Court. Governor Reubin Askew appointed McCrary secretary of state in 1978, making him also the first African American to serve in the Florida cabinet since Reconstruction.

FOR FURTHER READING: Susan MacManus, *Florida's Minority Trailblazers: The Men and Women Who Changed the Face of Florida Government* (Gainesville: University Press of Florida, 2017).

OCTOBER 30

On October 30, 1903, the *Weekly Tallahassean* published an account of the Florida State College football team's 5–0 victory over the Bainbridge Giants. The low-scoring event occurred in the football team's second year of existence. Prior to 1901, Florida State College had been known as the West Florida Seminary. Florida State College had no mascot or nickname, so its players were known as the Florida State College Eleven. Florida State College would later become the Florida College for Women and then Florida State University.

FOR FURTHER READING: Ric A. Kabat, "Before the Seminoles: Football at Florida State College, 1902–1904," *Florida Historical Quarterly* 70, no. 1 (1991): 20–37.

OCTOBER 31

On October 31, 1865, court martial proceedings began for six soldiers of the 3rd Regiment of the US Colored Troops in Jacksonville. They had engaged in a mutiny two days earlier in protest of the cruel punishment inflicted on a fellow soldier who had committed a petty act of thievery. African American soldiers frequently protested the use of torturous punishments that harkened back to plantation-style penalties. In this instance, the soldiers protested the Army's decision to string the convicted thief up by the thumbs. The six men were found guilty and were executed by a firing squad on December 1, 1865.

FOR FURTHER READING: John F. Fannin, "The Jacksonville Mutiny of 1865," *Florida Historical Quarterly* 88, no. 3 (2010): 368–396.

November

NOVEMBER 1

On November 1, 1841, Second Lieutenant William Tecumseh Sherman sank into poor spirits at Fort Pierce during the Second Seminole War, expressing his frustrations in a letter to his brother-in-law Philemon B. Ewing. Sherman served at the fort during a yellow fever outbreak, periods of severe weather, and what he considered incompetent command. His experiences in Florida, his first military post after the US Military Academy, led him to later adopt military strategies based on proper intelligence and command structure, swift action, and the taking or destroying of enemy resources. In many ways, his deployment of "hard war" tactics against civilians during the Civil War were first implemented by US officers fighting against the Seminoles in Florida.

FOR FURTHER READING: Jane F. Lancaster, "William Tecumseh Sherman's Introduction to War, 1840–1842: Lesson for Action," *Florida Historical Quarterly* 72, no. 1 (1993): 56–72.

November 2

On November 2, 1920, after weeks of threatening African American voters with violence if they tried to vote, white residents in Ocoee tried to stop a man from doing so. Mose Norman would not back down. He returned with a shotgun to secure his right to vote, and the white mob responded by burning the entire black section of the town to the ground. As many as seventy African Americans were killed during the massacre. Most African Americans fled the town afterward, making Ocoee essentially a whites-only community. One historian has since called this day the "single bloodiest day in modern American political history."

FOR FURTHER READING: Paul Ortiz, *Emancipation Betrayed: The Hidden History of Black Organizing and White Violence in Florida from Reconstruction to the Bloody Election of 1920* (Berkeley: University of California Press, 2005).

November 3

On November 3, 1957, pressure mounted on employees working on the Vanguard rocket program in Cocoa Beach as the Soviet Union launched *Sputnik 2*. It was the second spacecraft launched into Earth's orbit and the first to carry a living passenger; a dog named Laika did not return to Earth alive. The successful launch of *Sputnik 1* and then *Sputnik 2* convinced many in the US space program that it was losing the space race. Rushing to act months ahead of schedule, US engineers attempted to launch *Vanguard* from Cape Canaveral on December 6, 1957; the rocket rose only four feet in the air before it fell and exploded on impact.

FOR FURTHER READING: Lori C. Walters, "Beyond the Cape: An Examination of Cape Canaveral's Influence on the City of Cocoa Beach, 1950–1963," *Florida Historical Quarterly* 87, no. 2 (2008): 235–257.

On November 4, 1955, the Baptist Student Union of Stetson University proposed that the student body of the school officially support the integration of African American students within the next two years. Although the Baptist Student Union had nearly 300 members, almost a quarter of the student body, it was not a popular proposition among the rest of the students. It was defeated in a general election on December 2; the total number of votes against integration remained confidential. The administration agreed with the majority of its students, and Stetson did not integrate until 1962. Even with the delay, Stetson became one of the first Florida colleges to desegregate.

FOR FURTHER READING: Jason Blake, "The Integration of Stetson University," *Florida Historical Quarterly* 82, no. 4 (2004): 468–485.

November 5

On November 5, 1968, Florida voters approved a new state constitution. The public deliberated the new constitution without considering Article V, which deals with the judicial branch, because it was intentionally not submitted to the public. The 1968 Constitution is the sixth one to govern Florida and is the current one in place to date. The 1968 Constitution gave more political power to the voters, as it allowed citizens to bring amendments up for a vote through the petition process.

FOR FURTHER READING: Mary E. Adkins, *Making Modern Florida: How the Spirit of Reform Shaped a New State Constitution* (Gainesville: University Press of Florida, 2016).

PREAMBLE

We, the people of the State of Florida, being grateful to Almighty God for our constitutional liberty, in order to secure its benefits, perfect our government, insure domestic tranquility, maintain public order, and guarantee equal civil and political rights to all, do ordain and establish this constitution.

ARTICLE I

DECLARATION OF RIGHTS

Section 1. POLITICAL POWER.-- All political power is inherent in the people. The enunciation herein of certain rights shall not be construed to deny or impair others retained by the people.

Section 2. BASIC RIGHTS.-- All natural persons are equal before the law and have inalienable rights, among which are the right to enjoy and defend life and liberty, to pursue happiness, to be rewarded for industry, and to acquire, possess and protect property; except that the ownership, inheritance, disposition and possession of real property by aliens ineligible for citizenship may be regulated or prohibited by law. No person shall be deprived of any right because of race or religion.

Section 3. RELIGIOUS FREEDOM.-- There shall be no law respecting the establishment of religion or prohibiting or penalizing the free exercise thereof. Religious freedom shall not justify practices inconsistent with public morals, peace or safety. No revenue of the state or any political subdivision or agency thereof shall ever be taken from the public treasury directly or indirectly in aid of any church, sect, or religious denomination or in aid of any sectarian institution.

-1-   1-2x

On November 6, 1951, Lake County Sheriff Willis V. McCall shot African Americans Walter Irvin and Sam Shepherd as they awaited trial in connection to a likely specious rape accusation, an event since known as the Groveland Four case. McCall shot the two men as he was transferring them from Raiford State Prison. McCall claimed that he acted in self-defense against the two men, who were shackled in the back of a police car. Shepherd died at the scene. Though shot four times, Irvin survived. He testified that McCall shot him and Shepherd in cold blood. Nevertheless, authorities exonerated McCall and concluded that he was acting in the line of duty.

FOR FURTHER READING: Gilbert King, *Devil in the Grove: Thurgood Marshall, the Groveland Boys, and the Dawn of a New America* (New York: Harper, 2012).

On November 7, 1693, King Charles II of Spain declared that enslaved Africans who reached La Florida would receive their "liberty." The flight of enslaved men and women out of the British colonies began decades earlier, and Spanish authorities sought clarity on how to treat the fugitives. Ultimately, Spain encouraged them to form an independent community called Fort Mosé. The Spanish required that former slaves convert to Catholicism as well as the men to swear to serve the Spanish against any foreigners, which required four years of service in the Spanish army or militia. These former slaves were the front line of defense against invasions by the British and French. Eventually the African American settlement would have around a hundred residents; it was the first of its kind in America.

FOR FURTHER READING: Jane Landers, *Black Society in Spanish Florida* (Urbana: University of Illinois Press, 1999).

NOVEMBER 8

On November 8, 1973, construction on the new state capitol building began. It was completed in August 1977 and officially opened on March 31, 1978. The creation of a new building resulted from an effort to move the capital city away from Tallahassee and to a more centrally located city. The fight to move the capital backfired. It not only ensured the preservation of the historic old capitol but convinced the legislature that a new capitol building was needed. Rather than move the capital, lawmakers simply chose to rebuild the capitol. The building became the centerpiece of an entire capitol complex of more than twenty buildings that house the state's government offices. Lee Weissenborn, the state senator who fought to have to capital moved to Orlando, has a plaque in his honor in the capitol.

FOR FURTHER READING: David Colburn and Lance deHaven-Smith, *Government in the Sunshine State: Florida since Statehood* (Gainesville: University Press of Florida, 1999).

NOVEMBER 9

On November 9, 1964, the first meeting of the Governor's Commission on the Status of Women took place. The group of ten women had been appointed by Governor Haydon Burns, following in the footsteps of outgoing Governor Farris Bryant, whose idea the commission had been. The commission was chaired by Aleen Pridgen Kidd, who was also a national leader in highway safety. The commission made road and highway safety a priority in an era before seatbelts and airbags. Its main task, however, was to research inequalities faced by women throughout Florida, especially in legal and employment matters.

FOR FURTHER READING: Doris Weatherford, *They Dared to Dream: Florida Women Who Shaped History* (Gainesville: University Press of Florida, 2015).

NOVEMBER 10

On November 10, 1966, the Constitution Revision Commission finalized a draft of the revised state constitution that incorporated feedback and information from public hearings. The structure of the document would largely remain the same, though amendments were later added. The new constitution was needed because in 1964 and 1965, the courts ruled that the way Florida determined apportionment of state representatives was unconstitutional. It was unfair to newer, more populous districts. Prior to the 1968 Constitution, rural North Florida legislators had dominated the statehouse although they represented far fewer citizens than their South Florida colleagues.

FOR FURTHER READING: Mary E. Adkins, *Making Modern Florida: How the Spirit of Reform Shaped a New State Constitution* (Gainesville: University Press of Florida, 2016).

NOVEMBER 11

On November 11, 1828, the convicted mail robber Martin Hutto escaped custody in Pensacola. It was his fourth escape, and this one occurred only two days after he was sentenced to a two-year prison term.

The US Postal Service offered a $50 reward for his recapture, while the US Attorney for the Western Judicial District of Florida secured a total of twenty indictments and a fine of $106 against him. Hutto was a notorious criminal in territorial Florida, having made Pensacola and Escambia County's police look ridiculous and ineffectual with his easy escapes.

FOR FURTHER READING: James M. Denham, "Crime and Punishment in Antebellum Pensacola," *Florida Historical Quarterly* 90, no. 1 (2011): 13–33.

NOVEMBER 12

On November 12, 1937, Florida forester Harry Lee Baker sent a circular to Civilian Conservation Corps posts to declare fire suppression as the utmost of the CCC's duties. As a result, CCC workers devoted much of their time to putting out wildfires. Designed to put unskilled young men between the ages of eighteen and twenty-five to work during the Great Depression, the CCC employed around three million young men during its nine-year lifespan. The CCC also highlighted America's natural resources and the great outdoors.

Firebreak made by CCC workers in Washington County, ca. 1933.

FOR FURTHER READING: Dave Nelson, "'Improving' Paradise: The Civilian Conservation Corps and Environmental Change in Florida," in *Paradise Lost? The Environmental History of Florida*, ed. Jack E. Davis and Raymond Arsenault (Gainesville: University Press of Florida, 2005), 92–112.

NOVEMBER 13

On November 13, 1935, Director Harry L. Hopkins of the Federal Emergency Relief Agency declared that the Florida Keys needed rehabilitation to improve the economy. In a written response to the Florida governor's request for assistance from a recent hurricane, Hopkins made the recovery of the Keys a national priority. During the Great Depression, FERA took over management of the municipal finances of Key West and Monroe County and helped to rebuild a tourist industry that suffered from Prohibition and the recent growth of Miami. Hopkins tried to improve the islands' infrastructure and thereby bring tourism back to the area.

FOR FURTHER READING: Matthew G. Hyland, "The Florida Keys Hurricane House: Post-Disaster New Deal Housing," *Florida Historical Quarterly* 91, no. 2 (2012): 212–247.

NOVEMBER 14

On November 14, 1767, Juan Alonso Cabale died in Guanabaco, Cuba. Born in 1709 at a Spanish mission, Cabale was the last recognized Timucuan speaker at the time of his death. Living along the northern Florida and southeastern Georgia coasts, the Timucua numbered upward of 200,000 prior to European contact. As with other Native groups, the pressures of infectious disease, the Indian slave trade, and colonialism devastated the Timucua. As Spaniards abandoned their collapsing mission system, they frequently evacuated the Native Americans they had converted. As a result, Cabale passed away on an island far from his home.

FOR FURTHER READING: Jerald T. Milanich, *The Timucua* (Oxford, England: Blackwell, 1996).

NOVEMBER 15

On November 15, 1965, the plans for Disney World were officially announced at a press conference in Orlando. Present at the conference were Florida Governor Haydon Burns and Walt Disney himself. Disney had been secretly purchasing land in Central Florida through the use of dummy corporations to prevent the cost of land from going up. Disney kept many of the details of his project secret even after the announcement and only held a press conference after newspaper reporters doggedly pursued leads to find out who was buying up all the land.

FOR FURTHER READING: Derek R. Everett, "The Mouse and the Statehouse: Intersections of Florida's Capitols and Walt Disney World," *Florida Historical Quarterly* 96, no. 1 (2017): 63–94.

NOVEMBER 16

On November 16, 1987, the *St. Petersburg Times* declared that the state's new open-carry law posed a threat to tourist dollars. In an editorial with the headline "Gun Law Hurts Florida's Image," the newspaper took aim at a new law that allowed all citizens except "convicted felons, certified psychotics, and twice convicted drunks" to carry a handgun without a license as long as it was in plain sight. Newspapers across the country ran versions of the wire story; many cited the Miami resident quoted in the *St. Petersburg Times* saying he was moving back to Montana because Florida was not safe with the new law.

FOR FURTHER READING: Alison Meek, "Murders and Pastels in Miami: The Role of 'Miami Vice' in Bringing Back Tourists to Miami," *Florida Historical Quarterly* 90, no. 3 (2012): 286–305.

NOVEMBER 17

On November 17, 1973, during a press conference in Orlando, President Richard M. Nixon announced the five words that became synonymous with his presidency: "I am not a crook." Nixon tried to convince the journalists as well as the American people watching at home that he had not profited during his time in office, that he had earned everything he had, and that he had not obstructed justice. An investigation revealed otherwise, demonstrating that Nixon prevented the White House tapes from being turned over to investigators and agreed to pay the Watergate burglars for their work. Nixon resigned in August 1974.

FOR FURTHER READING: J. Brooks Flippen, *Nixon and the Environment* (Albuquerque: University of New Mexico Press, 2000).

NOVEMBER 18

On November 18, 1991, the convicted part-owner of Inair Airlines, Ricardo Bilonick, testified at the Miami trial of former Panamanian dictator General Manuel Noriega. Bilonick swore that Noriega was paid $500,000 for each of the nineteen Inair flights that smuggled cocaine to Miami in appliance shipments. The court convicted Noriega on eight of ten charges of drug trafficking, racketeering, and money laundering. In June 1992 he was sentenced to forty years in prison. He died in 2017 at the age of eighty-three of complications from brain surgery to remove a tumor.

FOR FURTHER READING: Steven Albert, *The Case against the General: Manuel Noriega and the Politics of American Justice* (New York: C. Scribner's Sons, 1993).

NOVEMBER 19

On November 19, 1979, film director Barry Jenkins was born in Miami. Jenkins attended college at Florida State University, where he studied film and earned a masters of fine arts degree in 2003. Jenkins became a household name with his 2016 film *Moonlight*, based on Tarell Alvin McCraney's play *In Moonlight Black Boys Look Blue*. The film tells the coming-of-age story of an African American boy struggling with his identity and sexuality, depicting his childhood, adolescence, and adulthood. Jenkins was nominated for an Oscar for Best Director for *Moonlight*; he was only the fourth African American to be nominated for the award. *Moonlight* and its cast were nominated for a total of eight Oscars and won Best Supporting Actor, Best Adapted Screenplay, and Best Picture. The Best Picture win was the second time a film directed by an African American won the coveted award.

FOR FURTHER READING: Mari Rich, "Barry Jenkins," *Current Biography* 78, no. 5, (May 2017): 39–44.

NOVEMBER 20

On November 20, 1831, John James Audubon arrived in St. Augustine to visit the plantation of John Bulow and explore the landscape around the St. Johns River. Audubon was a noted naturalist and ornithologist who produced highly detailed drawings and paintings of birds in the Americas. He eventually published these images in *The Birds of America*, a volume that is widely considered a classic of ornithology. Audubon traveled throughout the country and made multiple trips to Florida for some of the 497 species he depicted in the book.

FOR FURTHER READING: Kathryn Hall Proby, *Audubon in Florida: With Selections from the Writings of John James Audubon* (Coral Gables, FL: University of Miami Press, 1974).

On November 21, 1925, the Orange Blossom Special rail line began service. The luxury train line carried passengers from New York to Miami. It gained notoriety during the Roaring '20s when it earned the business of some of the wealthiest and prominent Americans in the winter months. When it first began, the Orange Blossom Special made the nearly 1,400-mile trip in thirty-five hours. Promotional materials boasted that its occupants could enjoy fine cuisine, full bars, and fancy flowers. Later, it was billed as the first train line with air-conditioned cars. Operated by the Seaboard Air Line, the Orange Blossom Special was quite popular with riders and the inspiration for a famous fiddle tune of the same name.

FOR FURTHER READING: Mark Wegman, *American Passenger Trains and Locomotives Illustrated* (Minneapolis, MN: Voyager, 2008).

NOVEMBER 22

On November 22, 1958, the University of Florida Gators defeated the Florida State University Seminoles in the first football game between the rival schools. The Gators, who won the game 21–7, initially were hesitant to play the Seminoles because they felt they had nothing to gain from playing a university that had only recently enrolled men and fielded a football team. For many years, UF officials insisted on playing at home, declaring that the FSU stadium was not a large enough venue to host the event. As a result, the first six games of the series were held in Gainesville. The series was uneven at the start also with UF dominating it for a couple of decades. By the 1990s the rivalry evened out, and the Thanksgiving-weekend game often has held championship implications.

FOR FURTHER READING: James P. Jones and Kevin M. McCarthy, *The Gators and the Seminoles: Honor, Guts, and Glory* (Gainesville: Maupin House, 1993).

NOVEMBER 23

On November 23, 1939, the state of Florida refused to observe the federal Thanksgiving holiday. That year President Franklin Roosevelt broke the custom of celebrating the holiday on the last Thursday of November. He shifted it one week earlier to jump-start the holiday shopping season and help businesses suffering from the Great

SARASOTA RETAIL MERCHANTS ASSOCIATION
SARASOTA, FLORIDA

October 26, 1939

Hon Fred P. Cone, Governor
State of Florida
Talahassee, Florida

Dear Govenor Cone:
    At a meeting of the Sarasota Retail Merchants
Association last Monday night, it was decided to adhere
to the date set by President Roosevelt for Thanksgiving
Day—that is November 23rd.

            Sincerely yours

            Sarasota Retail Merchants Assn.

            Secretary

Depression. Florida Governor Fred P. Cone refused to shun tradition in favor of shopping, and he declared November 30, 1939, as Florida's official state observance. Twenty-two other states did the same. The rest of the country observed "Franksgiving," as it was derisively called. Many Florida merchants disagreed with Governor Cone and observed Thanksgiving on November 23. To prevent confusion, in 1941 the US Congress declared the fourth Thursday in November as the nationwide observance.

FOR FURTHER READING: J. W. Baker, *Thanksgiving: The Biography of an American Holiday* (Durham, NH: University of New Hampshire Press, 2009).

NOVEMBER 24

On November 24, 1866, Tolly Harris, George Harris, and Jim Harris signed a labor contract with William H. H. Nichols in Jefferson County. After the Emancipation Proclamation, white landowners and southern politicians sought ways to maintain their control of the largely African American labor force. The contract the Harrises signed represents one of the many means white southerners used to limit the choices of freedmen and freedwomen. This contract and others like it obligated recently freed African Americans to work for landowners for an extended time. Those who left before their contracts expired faced criminal charges. Historians view freedmen contracts as another form of involuntary labor.

FOR FURTHER READING: Jerrell H. Shofner, *Nor Is It Over Yet: Florida in the Age of Reconstruction, 1863–1877* (Gainesville: University Press of Florida, 1974).

NOVEMBER 25

On Thanksgiving Day, November 25, 1999, five-year-old Cuban refugee Elián González and two others were rescued off Fort Lauderdale by the US Coast Guard. They had fled from Cuba with his mother and twelve refugees in a small boat. Elián's mother died while attempting to reach Florida, and so González was almost immediately thrust into a custody battle between his father in Cuba and relatives in Miami. Would Elián be reunited with his father in communist Cuba, or would he remain with family members that he just met in Miami? The fight caught the attention of the entire country as well as the world. The courts, which legally had to decide what was best for the child, ultimately returned Elián to his father.

FOR FURTHER READING: Alex Stepick, Guillermo Grenier, Max Castro, and Marvin Dunn, *This Land Is Our Land: Immigrants and Power in Miami* (Berkeley: University of California Press, 2003).

November 26

On November 26, 1934, administrators at Myakka State Park detailed efforts to improve the environment by removing natural flora and fauna in favor of ornamental plants. This approach typified that of many Americans at the time who sought to improve rather that preserve the natural world. Workers killed catfish, gar, and turtles, as it was believed that they competed with sport fish. They also removed native plants like longleaf pine and palmetto in favor of destructive and invasive plants like melaleuca and Australian pine. These misguided deeds at Myakka and other state parks continue to cause problems as the invasive species have overtaken native plants and animals in the region.

FOR FURTHER READING: Dave Nelson, "'Improving' Paradise: The Civilian Conservation Corps and Environmental Change in Florida," in *Paradise Lost? The Environmental History of Florida*, ed. Jack E. Davis and Raymond Arsenault (Gainesville: University Press of Florida, 2005), 304-322.

November 27

On November 27, 1656, Governor Diego de Rebolledo left St. Augustine to attend the trial of the Timucua chiefs who had revolted against the Spanish. The trial was held in the town of Ivitachuco. At the heart of the rebellion was a dispute over whether the Spanish Crown should press Indians into military service and extract their surplus food on behalf of the empire. The chiefs resisted both of these demands and thereby threw the Spanish system of rule into doubt. The Spanish found ten Timucua (six of them chiefs) guilty and sentenced them to death. In Florida and elsewhere in the Americas, Spain incorporated Indigenous people into its hierarchy, offering protection and salvation in return for labor and food. The Spanish Empire could not exist in Florida if the Timucua could resist these demands.

FOR FURTHER READING: Jerald T. Milanich, *The Timucua* (Malden, MA: Blackwell, 1996).

On November 28, 1966, civil rights activists began a boycott of the public schools in Leon County to protest Florida's reluctance to implement integration. Realizing that Florida distributed education monies based on attendance, civil rights attorney Kent Spriggs and education advocate Daisy Young announced a two-day boycott in which African American students would attend classes taught by volunteers at churches and community centers rather than attend their public schools. The boycott cost Leon County more than $20,000 in education reimbursement.

FOR FURTHER READING: Glenda Alice Rabby, *The Pain and the Promise: The Struggle for Civil Rights in Tallahassee* (Athens: University of Georgia Press, 1999).

November 29

On November 29, 1837, Coacoochee led an escape of several captured Seminoles from Fort Marion, the American name for the Castillo De San Marcos, in St. Augustine. Known to US officials as Wildcat, Coacoochee was the first victim of the Army's policy of ignoring flags of truce on the battlefield. After his escape, Coacoochee continued to fight for the ability of Native Americans to remain on their homelands in Florida. In many instances he fought alongside African Americans who feared that the war was nothing more than an extended slave raid. The US Army captured him again

Coacoochee. (Wild Cat.)

and forcibly removed him as well as his Seminole and African American allies to Indian Territory. Coacoochee's journey did not end there.

Rather than stay in Indian Territory, where slave raiders and others threatened his community, Coacoochee set up a new village in Mexico.

FOR FURTHER READING: Susan A. Miller, *Coacoochee Bones: A Seminole Saga* (Lawrence: University of Kansas Press, 2003).

NOVEMBER 30

On November 30, 1817, Native groups from northern Florida and southern Georgia attacked a US Army supply boat captained by Richard W. Scott as it ascended the Apalachicola River. The river was high due to heavy rains, forcing the boat to stay near the shore. This maneuver made the boat more vulnerable to the Seminole attack. The attack, which became known to Americans as the Scott massacre, was precipitated by the US military razing of the Creek village of Fowltown in Georgia a few days earlier. The events at Fowltown and on the Apalachicola River are often considered the beginning of the First Seminole War.

FOR FURTHER READING: John K. Mahon, "The First Seminole War, November 21, 1817–May 24, 1818," *Florida Historical Quarterly* 77, no. 1 (1998): 62–67.

December

DECEMBER 1

On December 1, 1963, Wendell Scott became the first African American to win a NASCAR race when he won the Jake 200 Grand National at Jacksonville Speedway. From Danville, Virginia, Scott served in World War II and began racing in the 1950s to promote his auto garage. Throughout his career, Scott experienced resistance and harassment from racing fans and other drivers. Despite winning the Jacksonville race by two laps, officials declared a white driver the winner. Without fanfare, Scott was awarded victory on an official appeal. He never received the winner's trophy.

FOR FURTHER READING: Daniel S. Pierce, *Real NASCAR: White Lightning, Red Clay, and Bill France* (Chapel Hill: University of North Carolina Press, 2010).

December 2

On December 2, 1839, Secretary of the Navy James K. Paulding advocated riverine attacks in the Everglades to capture Native women and children. By using light boats to go deeper into the Everglades, naval forces attacked Seminole homes and terrorized and captured Seminole families, hoping to bring an end to the Second Seminole War. The tactics were not very effective. Sailors rarely engaged with the enemy. Even when the US military discovered Indigenous camps in the interior, the Seminoles had usually abandoned their homes just prior to the arrival of US soldiers.

FOR FURTHER READING: R. Blake Dunnavent, "A Muddy Water Warrior's Manual: Toward a Riverine Warfare Tactical Doctrine in the Second Seminole War," *Florida Historical Quarterly* 78, no. 4 (2000): 417–429.

December 3

On December 3, 1948, Florida Governor Millard Caldwell advocated for southern states to cooperate in funding higher education. With Caldwell's advocacy, southern governors formed the Southern Education Regional Board, a plan to fund medical and professional schools for African American students. Meharry Medical College in Nashville, Tennessee, received the largest amount of the funds. For many years, the board explicitly used the funding of African American schools to help forestall the integration of higher education. Despite its origins, the SERB ultimately evolved into an advocate for integration.

FOR FURTHER READING: Karen Kruse Thomas, *Deluxe Jim Crow: Civil Rights and American Health Policy, 1935–1954* (Athens: University of Georgia Press, 2011).

DECEMBER 4

On December 4, 1954, the first franchised Burger King opened in Miami. It initially operated under the name Insta-Burger King. Owners James McLamore and David Edgerton rebranded it Burger King in 1959 and focused on a limited menu with fast service. After expanding their business to five locations in Miami, Burger King's owners franchised it by offering investors exclusive rights to large geographic areas. This approach followed a pattern similar to that of other fast-food innovators Ray Kroc of McDonald's and Harlan "Colonel" Sanders of Kentucky Fried Chicken.

FOR FURTHER READING: Ester Reiter, *Making Fast Food: From the Frying Pan into the Fryer* (Montreal: McGill-Queen's University Press, 1991).

DECEMBER 5

On December 5, 1963, Governor Farris Bryant defended President Lyndon B. Johnson's decision to rename Cape Canaveral as Cape Kennedy. The decision, done through Executive Order 11129, occurred after John F. Kennedy was assassinated in Dallas the month before. Bryant said that white Floridians might not understand the decision to honor a president committed to civil rights, but he declared that they would understand and appreciate the gesture in 2063. Kennedy had set a goal for the American people of reaching the lunar surface by 1970 and had been a proponent of the space program, visiting the site several times during his presidency.

FOR FURTHER READING: Kenneth Lipartito and Orville L. Butler, *A History of the Kennedy Space Center* (Gainesville: University Press of Florida, 2007).

DECEMBER 6

On December 6, 1947, Everglades National Park held its opening ceremony. The park was dedicated by President Harry S. Truman. Everglades National Park was conceived as a way to protect the Everglades environment from the rapid development occurring in South Florida.

The park was designated a UNESCO World Heritage Site in 1979; it now receives more than a million visitors every year. Only 20 percent of the original Everglades is inside the national park, but it is still the third-largest national park in the contiguous United States.

FOR FURTHER READING: Jack E. Davis, *An Everglades Providence: Marjory Stoneman Douglas and the American Environmental Century* (Athens: University of Georgia Press, 2009).

DECEMBER 7

On December 7, 1861, Captain James McKay revealed that despite the onset of the Civil War, Florida's cattle industry was alive and well. In a letter to US Army Adjutant General Lorenzo Thomas, he described how he had been shipping cattle from Tampa to Cuba nonstop. Perhaps in jest, he complained that he was so busy shipping cattle that he had not been home for ten days. McKay worked to secure as many "beeves" as possible in order to keep them out of Confederate hands. McKay had to act quickly, as he rightfully assumed that the United States would ultimately close the port to trade. McKay, an immigrant from Scotland, was a Unionist who hated to see the breakup of the country he had immigrated to as a young man.

FOR FURTHER READING: Canter Brown Jr., "Tampa's James McKay and the Frustration of Confederate Cattle-Supply Operations in South Florida," *Florida Historical Quarterly* 70, no. 4 (1992): 409–433.

DECEMBER 8

On December 8, 2000, the Florida Supreme Court, in a 4–3 ruling, ordered a manual recount of all "undervoted" ballots in Florida during the 2000 presidential election. The results would then be added to the vote tally from November 26. An undervote occurred when no vote for president had been machine-recorded and votes for lesser officers were recorded. The battle over the ballots thrust Florida into the world's spotlight because the razor-thin vote margin in the state would determine the balance of the electoral college. Other terms popularized during the vote count included "hanging chad" and "butterfly ballot." Florida had twenty-five electoral votes, enough to make either Republican George W. Bush or Democrat Al Gore president.

FOR FURTHER READING: Lance deHaven-Smith, ed., *The Battle for Florida: An Annotated Compendium of Materials from the 2000 Presidential Election* (Gainesville: University Press of Florida, 2005).

DECEMBER 9

On December 9, 1836, General Thomas S. Jesup declared that the Second Seminole War was "a negro, not an Indian war." In a letter to his superior in Washington, DC, he asserted that if the rebellion was not put down quickly, its effects would spread rapidly throughout the enslaved population in the South. Jesup later offered freedom to any African American fighting in the war if they agreed to move to Indian Territory. More than 600 men and women took the opportunity. Many of them left loved ones behind rather than risk enslavement by the US military.

FOR FURTHER READING: Andrew K. Frank, "Red, Black, and Seminole: Community Convergence on the Florida Borderlands," in *Borderland Narratives: Negotiation and Accommodation in North America's Contested Spaces, 1500–1850*, ed. Andrew K. Frank and A. Glenn Crothers (Gainesville: University Press of Florida, 2017), 46–67.

DECEMBER 10

On December 10, 1840, Chakaika, the leader of a Native community in southwestern Florida, was killed when the US military attacked his camp. The soldiers, disguised as Indians, attacked the community because Chakaika was thought to be responsible for a recent attack on a trading post on the Caloosahatchee River. Chakaika was known as a "Spanish Indian," widely seen as having Calusa as well as Spanish ancestry. The community traded and intermixed quite freely with Spanish fishermen and existed autonomously from other Indian communities on the Florida Peninsula. The United States targeted them and all Native Floridians for forced removal in the nineteenth century.

FOR FURTHER READING: John K. Mahon, *History of the Second Seminole War, 1835–1842* (Gainesville: University Press of Florida, 2017).

DECEMBER 11

On December 11, 1914, the townspeople of Fellsmere learned that Robert Kann, a new resident from Illinois, planned to build a large syrup mill on the shore of Blue Cypress Lake. Kann's intentions were announced in the *Fellsmere Tribune* as part of a larger campaign by boosters hoping to exploit eastern Central Florida's prime potential for growing and processing sugarcane. The history of sugarcane in the region stretches back to the sixteenth century, when early Spanish colonists introduced the crop to the region. Kann's syrup mill ultimately failed, though other sugar growers prospered later in the century in and around Fellsmere and elsewhere in Florida.

FOR FURTHER READING: Gordon Patterson, "Raising Cane and Refining Sugar: Florida Crystals and the Fame of Fellsmere," *Florida Historical Quarterly* 75, no. 4 (1997): 408–428.

DECEMBER 12

On December 12, 1740, Francisco Menendez petitioned the Spanish Crown for remuneration for his fidelity and leadership at Fort Mosé during the recent English invasion. An African previously enslaved in South Carolina, Menendez became a valuable ally to the Crown in the African American community that was established just to the west of St. Augustine. Without an answer, Menendez sailed to Spain to plead his case in person. He was captured at sea by the English and sold back into slavery in 1741. The wily Menendez somehow managed to escape his captors once again. He returned to Florida and his leadership position at Fort Mosé in 1752.

FOR FURTHER READING: Jane Landers, *Black Society in Spanish Florida* (Urbana: University of Illinois Press, 1999).

DECEMBER 13

On December 13, 1998, Kenneth H. "Buddy" MacKay took the oath of office as Florida governor in his office at the Capitol. He replaced Lawton Chiles, who died unexpectedly the previous day. Technically, MacKay became the governor immediately after Chiles's passing, but he was out of the state at the time and had to return to Florida before a swearing-in ceremony could take place. He served twenty-four days in the office before incoming governor-elect Jeb Bush assumed the office.

FOR FURTHER READING: Buddy MacKay, *How Florida Happened: The Political Education of Buddy MacKay* (Gainesville: University Press of Florida, 2010).

DECEMBER 14

On December 14, 1979, the Seminole Tribe of Florida opened its first bingo hall. The bingo parlor was constructed on the Hollywood Seminole reservation in Broward County. State and county officials attempted to shut down the bingo operations on the grounds that high-stakes gambling was illegal in the state. As the jackpots grew, so did the opposition. The dispute ended up in federal court, where the judges established the basis for tribal gaming in the US. The ruling followed the Seminoles' argument that the bingo parlor operated on sovereign land, did not break any criminal laws as the state already allowed various forms of gambling, and therefore did not need to follow local civil codes that regulated the hours and stakes of the gaming.

FOR FURTHER READING: Jessica R. Cattelino, *High Stakes: Florida Seminole Gaming and Sovereignty* (Durham, NC: Duke University Press, 2008).

December 15

On December 15, 1921, Martin Tabert was arrested in Leon County and charged with vagrancy for illegally riding a train. A laborer from North Dakota, Tabert was traveling through Florida on an extended trip through the country. After his arrest he was sent to Putnam Lumber Company in Dixie County to work off his vagrancy fine. The punishment was a common occurrence in the convict-lease system in the early twentieth century. Tabert's family wired funds for his release, yet he suffered severe physical abuse at the labor camp. Ultimately, a camp employee whipped Tabert to death for failing to complete his work. Tabert's torturous  demise received national media attention and led to the end of the convict-lease system in Florida.

FOR FURTHER READING: Matthew J. Mancini, *One Dies, Get Another: Convict Leasing in the American South, 1866–1928* (Columbia: University of South Carolina Press, 1996).

DECEMBER 16

On December 16, 1978, the Florida A&M University Rattlers won the inaugural Division 1-AA college football championship. Led by Coach Rudy Hubbard, FAMU defeated the University of Massachusetts, Amherst, 35–28. Since then, FAMU football has been selected by voters as historically black colleges and universities (HBCUs) national champion on several other occasions, most recently in 2010. FAMU has a long history of distinguished football teams. Prior to the desegregation of college sports, many considered it to have one of the finest programs in the country. After integration, FAMU and other HBCUs ceased to attract many of the top African American athletes.

FOR FURTHER READING: Derrick E. White, *Blood, Sweat, and Tears: Hank Gaither, Florida A&M, and the History of Black College Football* (Chapel Hill: University of North Carolina Press, 2019).

DECEMBER 17

On December 17, 1913, Thomas Wesley Benoist signed a contract for commercial passenger air service. His agreement with the St. Petersburg Board of Trade was the first of its kind. An innovative aviator and airplane manufacturer, Benoist used his flying boats to connect St. Petersburg and Tampa from January to May 1914. The St. Petersburg–Tampa Airboat Line carried passengers across the bay without any notable accidents. Despite its safety record and utility, it was not financially successful. Benoist shut down the operation shortly after his contract ran out.

FOR FURTHER READING: Beverly Huttinger, *Florida Firsts: The Famous, Infamous, and Quirky of the Sunshine State* (Philadelphia: Camino, 2002).

DECEMBER 18

On December 18, 1888, James Dean was commissioned as a judge for Monroe County. A graduate of Howard Law School, Dean was the first African American county judge in Florida. He did not hold his

position for long. Using an erroneous charge that Dean issued a marriage license to an interracial couple, Governor Francis Fleming forced Dean to resign in 1889. Many residents of Key West petitioned the governor on his behalf, but it was of no avail. Governor Jeb Bush restored Dean's position posthumously in 2002.

FOR FURTHER READING: Canter Brown Jr. and Larry E. Rivers, "The Pioneer African American Jurist Who Almost Became a Bishop: Florida's Judge James Dean, 1858–1914," *Florida Historical Quarterly* 87, no. 1 (2008): 16–49.

DECEMBER 19

On December 19, 1960, NASA successfully launched a Mercury-Redstone rocket into orbit from Cape Canaveral. The flight was not occupied. After orbiting, the capsule returned to Earth using parachutes to slow its descent. The flight opened the way for continuation of the astronaut program. It was a significant step forward over the first Mercury-Redstone launch test in November 1960. The earlier attempt was an embarrassing failure. Its rocket engines shut off immediately after launch, and it lifted off only a few inches before settling back on the launch pad.

FOR FURTHER READING: John C. Fredriksen, *The United States Air Force: A Chronology* (Santa Barbara, CA: ABC-CLIO, 2011).

DECEMBER 20

On December 20, 1908, Frank Stoneman wrote a blistering critique of Governor Napoleon Bonaparte Broward's policies to drain the Everglades. In an editorial in the *Miami Morning News-Record*, he claimed that the governor's policies were unscientific and had changed significantly from those Broward expressed while still a gubernatorial candidate. Though not initially opposed to drainage, Stoneman was critical of Broward's unscientific and inefficient approach to the project. Stoneman eventually became a supporter of the creation of Everglades National Park in the 1930s.

FOR FURTHER READING: Chris Wilhelm, "Pragmatism, Seminoles, and Science: Opposition to Progressive Everglades Drainage," *Florida Historical Quarterly* 90, no. 4 (2012): 426–452.

DECEMBER 21

On December 21, 1979, Arthur McDuffie died from several fractures to his skull. The Miamian and African American was fatally wounded at the hands of police after a traffic chase four days earlier. Riots engulfed parts of Miami when the four officers who killed McDuffie were found not guilty by an all-white jury on May 17, 1980. The community's response to the acquittal of the officers revealed the anger and frustrations over police misconduct in South Florida. Miami-Dade later settled a civil case with McDuffie's family.

FOR FURTHER READING: T. D. Allman, *Finding Florida: The True History of the Sunshine State* (New York: Atlantic Monthly, 2013).

DECEMBER 22

On December 22, 1956, the Tallahassee bus boycott ended after eight months. The boycott began in May when two African American students from Florida A&M University, Wilhelmina Jakes and Carrie Patterson, tried to sit in seats designated for whites only on a Tallahassee bus. The boycott sought to desegregate buses as well as secure jobs for African American bus drivers in the state capital. Although locally organized, it received help from the NAACP and CORE (Congress on Racial Equality). Both goals were met by 1959.

FOR FURTHER READING: Glenda Alice Rabby, *The Pain and the Promise: The Struggle for Civil Rights in Tallahassee* (Athens: University of Georgia, 1999).

DECEMBER 23

On December 23, 1856, the county of Lafayette was created. It was posthumously named for Gilbert du Motier, the marquis de Lafayette, because of his enduring love and support for the United States. During Lafayette's last visit to America in 1824–1825 he went to every state. Although he never saw the territory of Florida, the US Congress granted Lafayette a large piece of land east of Tallahassee as a token of admiration. It was known as the Lafayette Land Grant. Today it is known as Frenchtown.

FOR FURTHER READING: George B. Utley, "Origin of the County Names in Florida," *Publications of the Florida Historical Society* 1, no. 3 (1908): 29–35.

DECEMBER 24

On December 24, 1894, Florida faced the first of a series of three severe freezes that struck the state that winter. During what was known as the Great Freeze, unusually cold temperatures killed citrus and native palm trees throughout most of the state. The Great Freeze prompted many investors and would-be citrus growers to reconsider thoughts of putting their resources into Florida. Julia Tuttle, who lived at the mouth of the Miami River, persuaded the otherwise hesitant Standard Oil magnate Henry M. Flagler to extend his East Coast Railway southward. Her gift of an orange blossom from Miami, and an offer to allow Flagler to put his hotel on her land, sealed the deal. This ultimately resulted in the establishment of the city of Miami and its growth into a metropolis. It also earned Flagler the nickname "Father of Miami" and Tuttle the nickname of "Mother of Miami."

FOR FURTHER READING: Arva Parks and Carolyn Klepser, *Miami: Then and Now* (London: Pavilion, 2014).

December 25

On December 25, 1951, Harry T. Moore was assassinated by white supremacists in his home in Seminole County. He died during a thirty-mile trip to the closest African American hospital. Moore's wife, Harriette, was also mortally injured in the bombing and passed away on January 3, 1952. The Moores were both educators and civil rights activists in mid-twentieth-century Florida. Among his many leadership positions, Harry Moore was the founder of the Brevard County chapter and president of the Florida chapter of the NAACP. The FBI investigated the assassination, but no charges were ever brought.

FOR FURTHER READING: Ben Green and Stetson Kennedy, *Before His Time: The Untold Story of Harry T. Moore, America's First Civil Rights Martyr* (New York: Free Press, 1999).

December 26

On December 26, 1912, the *Havana Daily Post* reported on the University of Florida football team's 27–0 victory over the Cuban Vedado Tennis Club. The game took place in Cuba as part of a campaign to pit US collegiate teams against the best American-style football team from Cuba. The victory surprised many. The Cuban team already had defeated Tulane and narrowly lost to Mississippi A&M (now Mississippi

State University) in similar games. The Gators and several other collegiate teams were given an all-expenses trip to Cuba to play against the home team.

FOR FURTHER READING: Michael T. Wood, "'Gators Making Merry in Cuba': The University of Florida Football Team in Havana, December 1912," *Historical Quarterly* 94, no. 1 (2015): 68–91.

DECEMBER 27

On December 27, 1975, a crowd of 15,202 assembled at the Miami Jai Alai Fronton. It was the largest crowd ever to watch jai alai, a fast-paced game originating in the Basque region of Spain. Jai alai was long a popular spectator activity in Florida and allowed on-site wagering. The popularity of the sport has significantly declined with the legalization of other forms of gaming in Florida. Today most of Florida's frontons make more money from their poker rooms than from jai alai.

FOR FURTHER READING: Josh Chetwynd, *The Secret History of Balls: The Stories behind the Things We Love to Catch, Whack, Throw, Kick, Bounce, and Bat* (New York: TarcherPerigee, 2011).

DECEMBER 28

On December 28, 1835, Native Americans resisting federal Indian-removal policies carried out coordinated attacks that officially instigated the Second Seminole War. A group of Seminoles led by Osceola killed US Indian agent Wiley Thompson at Fort King. Micanopy led another group of Native Americans in an ambush of Francis Dade's column of 110 US soldiers. The Seminoles killed all but two of Dade's men as they were marching from Fort Brooke to Fort King. The two attacks were precipitated by the insistence that the Seminoles leave their homelands.

FOR FURTHER READING: John K. Mahon, *History of the Second Seminole War, 1835–1842* (Gainesville: University Press of Florida, 2017).

DECEMBER 29

On December 29, 1687, construction halted on the Castillo de San Marcos in St. Augustine because of a lack of supplies and overburdening of the Native labor force. Spanish officials relied heavily on Natives to provide labor and food, and by 1687 their communities were stretched thin. As a result, Spanish officials brought enslaved Africans and English prisoners to help work on the fort. The coordination of the work was especially difficult because of the cultural and linguistic differences among the workers. In addition to Spaniards, Englishmen, and Africans, the Indigenous workers came from distinctive communities in Florida. The Guale, Timucua, and Apalachee spoke different languages and brought their own intertribal tensions with them.

FOR FURTHER READING: Jason B. Palmer, "Forgotten Sacrifice: Native American Involvement in the Construction of the Castillo de San Marcos," *Florida Historical Quarterly* 80, no. 4 (2002): 437–454.

DECEMBER 30

On December 30, 1842, Josiah T. Walls was born into slavery in Virginia. He escaped and joined the Union Army during the Civil War. He was ultimately discharged in Florida. After serving Alachua County in state politics, he became the first African American to represent Florida in the US House of Representatives. He served from 1871 to 1875. He lost reelection to the House in 1874 and served Alachua County in the Florida Senate from 1877 to 1881. He died in 1905.

FOR FURTHER READING: Peter D. Klingman, *Josiah Walls: Florida's Black Congressman of Reconstruction* (Gainesville: University Press of Florida, 1976).

DECEMBER 31

On December 31, 1938, the Florida State Board of Health's annual report included information on the newly created division of Venereal Disease Control. Venereal disease became a serious health concern in the years leading up to World War II. In 1938 at least 1,122 cases of venereal disease were reported in the United States, and the disease became a national concern. The creation of a division devoted to fighting venereal diseases recognized the particular threat to the state. The issue was especially pronounced near military bases through prostitution and "sporting houses" where the diseases more easily spread. As the military built new bases in Florida, health officials rightfully feared that cases of venereal disease would increase as well.

FOR FURTHER READING: Claire Strom, "Controlling Venereal Disease in Orlando during World War II," *Florida Historical Quarterly* 91, no. 1 (2012): 86–117.

ILLUSTRATION CREDITS

Page 1: Ruins of a burned African American home—Rosewood, Florida. 1923. Black & white photoprint, 4 × 10 in. State Archives of Florida, Florida Memory.

Page 2: Footbridge at the Cypress Gardens theme park in Winter Haven, Florida. 195-. Color slide. State Archives of Florida, Florida Memory.

Page 4: Winston Churchill painting at the Surf Club—Miami Beach, Florida. 1946. Black & white photoprint, 10 × 8 in. State Archives of Florida, Florida Memory.

Page 7: A chain gang for collecting scrape. 191-. Black & white photoprint, 8 × 10 in. State Archives of Florida, Florida Memory.

Page 9: Mary Catherine Lawhon Kahn. Between 1943 and 1945. Black & white photonegative, 5 × 4 in. State Archives of Florida, Florida Memory.

Page 10: Hotel Royal Palm [i.e. Royal Palm Hotel], Miami, Fla. Library of Congress Prints and Photographs Division, Washington, D.C.

Page 12: Tampa Bay on the Gulf of Mexico. 1937. Library of Congress Prints and Photographs Division Washington, D.C.

Page 15: Al Capone—Miami Beach, Florida. 19—. Black & white photoprint, 10 × 8 in. State Archives of Florida, Florida Memory.

Page 16: Civil rights activists—Tallahassee, Florida. Not before 1957. Black & white photoprint, 8 × 10 in. State Archives of Florida, Florida Memory.

Page 18: Painting of Seminole Chief Osceola by George Catlin. 1837. Black & white photoprint, 10 × 8 in. State Archives of Florida, Florida Memory.

Page 20: Bok Tower—Lake Wales, Florida. Between 1935 and 1936. Black & white photoprint, 10 × 8 in. State Archives of Florida, Florida Memory.

Page 22: Remington, Frederic, 1861–1909. *A Cracker Cowboy*. 1895. Black & white photoprint, 10 × 8 in. State Archives of Florida, Florida Memory.

Page 24: Announcement of a slave auction in Jacksonville, 1856. State Archives of Florida, Florida Memory.

Page 25: Portrait of author Ernest Hemingway posing with sailfish Key West, Florida. Wikicommons, https://commons.wikimedia.org/wiki/File:Portrait_of_author_Ernest_Hemingway_posing_with_sailfish_Key_West,_Florida.jpg.

Page 26: Bill Clinton and Janet Reno, half-length, standing, facing each other, [19]93. Official White House photograph. No. P002532-22A. Prints & Photographs Online Catalog, Library of Congress.

Page 27: James Weldon Johnson. 19—. Black & white photoprint, 10 × 8 in. State Archives of Florida, Florida Memory.

Page 29: Convicted killer, Theodore Bundy. 198-?. Black & white photonegative, 4 × 5 in. State Archives of Florida, Florida Memory.

Page 30: Panton Leslie & Company headquarters—Pensacola, Florida. 19—?. Black & white photonegative, 4 × 5 in. State Archives of Florida, Florida Memory.

Page 32: Kerce, Red (Benjamin L.), 1911–1964. Family of Sergeant Ernest Thomas looking at display case. 1945. Black & white photoprint, 8 × 10 in. State Archives of Florida, Florida Memory.

Page 34: Championship fight of Clay and Liston—Miami Beach, Florida. 1964. Black & white photoprint, 8 × 10 in. State Archives of Florida, Florida Memory.

Page 39: Act Establishing Florida Statehood, 1845. State Archives of Florida: Collection M81–22. State Archives of Florida, Florida Memory.

Page 41: Flier for Jackie Robinson's appearance at Greater Bethel A.M.E. Church in Miami on September 1, 1960. State Archives of Florida, Florida Memory.

Page 42: Sir Malcolm Campbell's Blue Bird II. 193-. Black & white photonegative, 4 × 5 in. State Archives of Florida, Florida Memory.

Page 44: Stainer, Don. Virgil Hawkins speaks with supporters during recess—Tallahassee, Florida. 1983. Black & white photoprint, 8 × 10 in. State Archives of Florida, Florida Memory.

Page 45: The Patriot Constitution of 1812. State Archives of Florida, Florida Memory.

Page 48: CORE press release about five jailed student leaders receiving Gandhi Award, 1960, State Archives of Florida, Florida Memory.

Page 50: Nyberg, Rindy. View of cars and visitors on the beach during Spring Break in Daytona Beach, Florida. Between 1976 and 1996. Color slide. State Archives of Florida, Florida Memory.

Page 52: "Hunting Indians in Florida." WikiCommons. https://commons.wikimedia.org/wiki/File:Hunting_Indians_in_Florida.jpg

Page 55: Foley, Mark T., 1943-. Widow Teresa Earnhardt watching Governor Bush sign the Earnhardt Family Protection Act—Tallahassee, Florida. 2001. Color digital image. State Archives of Florida, Florida Memory

Page 56: Etching of a shipwreck. 1864. Black & white photonegative, 4 × 5 in. State Archives of Florida, Florida Memory.

Page 59: Tamiami trail blazers holding sign—Tamiami Trail, Florida. 1923. Black & white photoprint, 8 × 10 in. State Archives of Florida, Florida Memory.

Page 60: Painting of William Augustus Bowles. 1790. Black & white photoprint, 10 × 8 in. State Archives of Florida, Florida Memory.

Page 62: Marjorie Kinnan Rawlings—Cross Creek, Florida. 194-. Black & white photoprint, 8 × 10 in. State Archives of Florida, Florida Memory.

Page 63: Grant, A. G. Governor Marcellus L. Stearns greeting Harriet Beecher Stowe on the steps of the Capitol. 1874. Sepia photoprint, 16 × 20 in. State Archives of Florida, Florida Memory.

Page 64: "You Can't Fool Mother Nature—Stop the ERA," pamphlet. State Archives of Florida, Florida Memory.

Page 65: McDonald, Dale M., 1949–2007. The *El Dorado* packed with Cuban refugees during the Mariel Boatlift—Key West, Florida. 1980. Color digital image. State Archives of Florida, Florida Memory.

Page 67: Chloe Merrick Reed. 18—. Black & white photonegative, 4 × 5 in. State Archives of Florida, Florida Memory.

Page 70: Dept. of Customs and Immigration identification card for a Conch Republic registered customs agent—Key West, Floridarealia. 19—. Color identification card, 3 × 4 in. State Archives of Florida, Florida Memory.

Page 72: Slave deck of the bark *Wildfire* brought into Key West. 1860. Black & white photonegative, 3 × 5 in. State Archives of Florida, Florida Memory.

Page 73: The trial of Ambrister during the Seminole War—Florida. 1848. Black & white photoprint, 8 × 10 in. State Archives of Florida, Florida Memory.

Page 75: Portrait of Florida representative Mary Lou Baker. ca 1943. Black & white photonegative, 4 × 5 in. State Archives of Florida, Florida Memory.

Page 76: Remains of the courthouse and armory, after the Fire of 1901—Jacksonville, Florida. 1901. Black & white photonegative, 4 × 5 in. State Archives of Florida, Florida Memory.

Page 77: Michael, Nancy, Collector. Painting by Robert Butler of Seminole Polly Parker. 1989. Color slide. State Archives of Florida, Florida Memory.

Page 78: Shannon, Frank. Portrait of Dr. Gorrie—Dr. John Gorrie historic memorial. 19—. Color postcard, 9 × 14 cm. State Archives of Florida, Florida Memory.

Page 82: Orange Bowl demolition. Wikicommons, https://commons.wikimedia.org/wiki/File:Trashed_bowl_(2484559507).jpg

Page 85: Mary McLeod Bethune. 1951?. Black & white photonegative, 4 × 5 in. State Archives of Florida, Florida Memory.

Page 86: Brockmann, Sara. Reenactors re-create a reading of the Emancipation Proclamation at the Knott House Museum in Tallahassee. 2015. Color digital image. State Archives of Florida, Florida Memory.

Page 87: Louise R. Pinnell. 19—. Black & white photonegative, 4 × 5 in. State Archives of Florida, Florida Memory.

Page 89: Saint Augustine Map. 1589. State Archives of Florida, Florida Memory.

Page 92: Ringling Brothers circus poster. 1897. Black & white photograph, 8 × 10 in. State Archives of Florida, Florida Memory.

Page 93: Harris & Ewing. Amelia Earhart, *left*. 1936. Library of Congress, Washington D.C. https://www.loc.gov/item/2016882726/

Page 94: Representative Maxine E. Baker. Between 1963 and 1972. Black & white photonegative, 7 × 5 in. State Archives of Florida, Florida Memory.

Page 98: Martin Luther King Jr. being escorted away from the Grand Jury in St. Augustine, Florida. 1964?. Black & white digital image. State Archives of Florida, Florida Memory.

Page 99: Davison, Judi, 1965–. Pulse nightclub sign in Orlando. 2016. Color digital image. State Archives of Florida, Florida Memory.

Page 101: United States Marshal branding the author. 18—. Black & white photoprint, 7 × 10 in. State Archives of Florida, Florida Memory.

Page 102: Segregationists trying to prevent blacks from swimming at a "white only" beach in St. Augustine. 1964. Black & white photoprint, 8 × 10 in. State Archives of Florida, Florida Memory.

Page 104: Lithograph of Fort Caroline. ca 1670. Black & white photoprint, 8 × 10 in. State Archives of Florida, Florida Memory.

Page 105: "Conquistadors and Missionaries." 19—. Black & white photonegative, 1 × 1 in. State Archives of Florida, Florida Memory.

Page 109: Entrance to the Arthur G. Dozier School in Marianna, Florida. Not before 1967. Color photoprint, 4 × 5 in. State Archives of Florida, Florida Memory.

Page 113: Mrs. Farris Bryant arriving at premiere of Elvis Presley's *Follow that* Dream—Ocala, Florida. Between 1961 and 1965. Black & white photoprint, 10 × 8 in. State Archives of Florida, Florida Memory.

Page 115: "A View of the Town and Castle of St. Augustine." State Archives of Florida, Florida Memory.

Page 117: Portrait of princess Catherine Willis Gray Murat—Tallahassee, Florida. 18—. Black & white photoprint, 10 × 8 in. State Archives of Florida, Florida Memory.

Page 119: Apollo 11 take off. 1969. Color photograph, 7 × 11 in. State Archives of Florida, Florida Memory.

Page 121: Holland, Karl E., 1919–1993. Children with Snooty the manatee at the South Florida Museum—Bradenton, Florida. 1976. Black & white photoprint, 8 × 10 in. State Archives of Florida, Florida Memory.

Page 122: Jo and Sada Sakai of Yamato. ca 1910. Black & white photograph, 8 × 10 in. State Archives of Florida, Florida Memory.

Page 123: Civil rights demonstration at Fort Lauderdale's segregated public beach. 1961. Black & white photonegative, 4 × 5 in. State Archives of Florida, Florida Memory.

Page 126: Telegram from Jessie Daniel Ames to Governor Sholtz, 1934. State Archives of Florida, Florida Memory.

Page 128: Underwater archaeologist investigating wrecked ship off Florida Keys—Lower Matecumbe Key, Florida. 19—. Black & white photograph, 8 × 10 in. State Archives of Florida, Florida Memory.

Page 131: Hastings. Jai alai players play at a jai alai frontons—Quincy, Florida. 1980. Black & white photoprint, 3 × 3 in. State Archives of Florida, Florida Memory.

Page 133, top: Group at segregated beach—Virginia Key, Florida. 1945. Black & white photonegative, 4 × 5 in. State Archives of Florida, Florida Memory.

Page 133, bottom: William V. Knott, Florida Comptroller. Between 1912 and 1917. Black & white photonegative, 4 × 5 in. State Archives of Florida, Florida Memory.

Page 134: Portrait of author Zora Neale Hurston. 19—. Black & white photoprint, 4 × 3 in. State Archives of Florida, Florida Memory.

Page 135: Bujak, David. Debris from structures destroyed by Hurricane Charley—Punta Gorda, Florida. 2004. Color digital image. State Archives of Florida, Florida Memory.

Page 136: Engraving of John Horse. ca 1842. Black & white photoprint, 10 × 8 in. State Archives of Florida, Florida Memory.

Page 137: Artist's sketch of Tristan de Luna—Pensacola, Florida. 1959. Black & white photoprint, 5 × 4 in. State Archives of Florida, Florida Memory.

Page 139: Florida State Senator Lawton Mainor Chiles Jr. walking on side of road during campaign for U.S. Senate. 1970. Color photoprint, 8 × 10 in. State Archives of Florida, Florida Memory.

Page 140: Kitchen and main house at the Kingsley Plantation State Park on Fort George Island in Jacksonville, Florida. 195-. Black & white photoprint, 8 × 10 in. State Archives of Florida, Florida Memory.

Page 142: Ferguson, Caroline. Entrance to council house at the San Luis Mission—Tallahassee, Florida. 2005. Color digital image. State Archives of Florida, Florida Memory.

Page 143: Damage from Hurricane Cleo—Miami, Florida. 1964. Black & white photoprint, 8 × 10 in. State Archives of Florida, Florida Memory.

Page 144: "The Promontory of Florida, at Which the French Touched; Named by Them the French Promontory." Theodor de Bry engravings, 1591. State Archives of Florida, Florida Memory.

Page 146: Johnson, Francis P. Tourists walking through the drawbridge between the main fortress and a ravelin—Saint Augustine, Florida. 1953. Black & white photoprint, 4 × 5 in. State Archives of Florida, Florida Memory.

Page 148: "In the Ghastly Wake of the Hurricane." 1935. Black & white photonegative, 3 × 5 in. State Archives of Florida, Florida Memory.

Page 149: "A correct map of the United States of North America; including the British and Spanish territories, carefully laid down agreeable to the treaty of 1784." State Archives of Florida, Florida Memory.

Page 151: Dughi, Donn (Donald Gregory), 1932–2005. Treasure hunter Mel Fisher of Treasure Salvors viewing item retrieved from the Atocha ship wreck—Tallahassee, Florida. 1978. Black & white photonegative, 35 mm. State Archives of Florida, Florida Memory.

Page 152: First permanent European settlement in the United States. 19—. Black & white photograph, 8 × 10 in. State Archives of Florida, Florida Memory.

Page 153: Dahlgren, Robert E. Florida Citrus Commission poster. 1944. Black & white photoprint, 5 × 7 in. State Archives of Florida, Florida Memory.

Page 154, top: Barchard, Vern. Beatles giving a press conference at the George Washington Hotel in Jacksonville. 1964. Black & white digital image. State Archives of Florida, Florida Memory.

Page 154, bottom: Gemini 11 lift off. 1966. Black & white photograph, 8 × 10 in. State Archives of Florida, Florida Memory.

Page 157: Drawn portrait of Andrew Ellicott. 18——. Black & white photonegative, 3 × 5 in. State Archives of Florida, Florida Memory.

Page 158: Barron, Charles Lee, 1917–1997. Flipper (Mitzi) leaping through hoop—Marathon, Florida. 1966. Black & white photoprint, 5 × 4 in. State Archives of Florida, Florida Memory.

Page 159: Engraving of massacre at Fort Caroline. 1562. Black & white photoprint, 8 × 10 in. State Archives of Florida, Florida Memory.

Page 160, top: Painting of Alvar Nunez Cabeza de Vaca on postage stamp. 15——. Black & white photoprint, 10 × 8 in. State Archives of Florida, Florida Memory.

Page 160, bottom: Governor LeRoy Collins delivering inaugural address—Tallahassee, Florida. 1957. Black & white photoprint, 10 × 8 in. State Archives of Florida, Florida Memory.

Page 163: Juan Ponce de León from Herrera's *Historia General*, published between 1601 and 1615. "Juan Ponce de León Lands in Florida," The Florida Memory Blog, April 2, 2013.

Page 166: Plan of Castillo de San Marcos. 1675. Black & white photograph, 8 × 10 in. State Archives of Florida, Florida Memory.

Page 167: State Normal and Industrial College for Colored Students. ca 1897. Black & white photonegative, 3 × 5 in. State Archives of Florida, Florida Memory.

Page 168: Portrait of folklorist and author Stetson Kennedy. 19——. Black & white photoprint, 10 × 8 in. State Archives of Florida, Florida Memory.

Page 170: A few of the school seaplanes and hangars at U.S.N. Air Station. Not after 1919. Hand-colored souvenir viewbook, 9 × 14 cm. State Archives of Florida, Florida Memory.

Page 171: Bartram, William, 1739–1823. Photograph of a drawing by William Bartram of two alligators in the St. Johns River. 1773 or 1774. Black & white photograph, 8 × 10 in. State Archives of Florida, Florida Memory.

Page 172: Drawing of Jean Ribault and his troops. 15——. Black & white photoprint, 10 × 8 in. State Archives of Florida, Florida Memory.

Page 175: Wikicommons, https://commons.wikimedia.org/wiki/File:Reefer_Madness_(1936).jpg

Page 177: Drawing of Pedro Menendez de Aviles. 1565. Black & white photoprint, 10 × 8 in. State Archives of Florida, Florida Memory.

Page 179: Luoma, Steve. Key Haven housing community street flooded during Hurricane Wilma—Key West, Florida. 2005. Color digital image. State Archives of Florida, Florida Memory

Page 180: San Marco Avenue entrance to the Fountain of Youth, St. Augustine, Fla. 19——. Hand-colored postcard, 9 × 14 cm. State Archives of Florida, Florida Memory.

Page 181: Telegram from Walter White to Governor Sholtz on imminent lynching of Claude Neal, 1934. State Archives of Florida, Florida Memory.

Page 182: Poster showing the various insignia used by the divisions of the Office of Civilian Defense and their subsidiaries throughout the United States during World War II. State Archives of Florida: Series S1205, Box 01, Folder 11.

Page 183: Jesse J. McCrary Jr. with Governor Askew just prior to taking the oath of office—Tallahassee, Florida. 1978. Black & white photoprint, 8 × 9 in. State Archives of Florida, Florida Memory

Page 187: Page 1 of the 1968 Florida Constitution. 1968. Black & white photoprint, 9 × 5 in. State Archives of Florida, Florida Memory

Page 188: Stop This Murder! N.A.A.C.P. Pamphlet, 1951. State Archives of Florida, Florida Memory

Page 191: Twenty foot fire break made by the C.C.C.—Washington County, Florida. 1933 or 1934. Black & white photoprint, 10 × 8 in. State Archives of Florida, Florida Memory.

Page 193: Walt Disney, Governor Burns, and Roy Disney at a press conference in Orlando, Florida. 1965. Black & white photoprint, 4 × 5 in. State Archives of Florida, Florida Memory.

Page 195: Audubon, John James, 1785–1851. Flamingo drawing. 1832. Black & white photoprint, 7 × 5 in. State Archives of Florida, Florida Memory.

Page 196: Fohl, Robert, Sr. Orange Blossom Special arrives in Naples. 1927. Black & white photoprint, 8 × 10 in. State Archives of Florida, Florida Memory.

Page 197: Letter from P.M. Birmingham to Governor Fred P. Cone Regarding the Date of Thanksgiving, October 26, 1939. State Archives of Florida, Florida Memory.

Page 198: Contract Between William H.H. Nichols & Tolly Harris, George Harris, et.al. State Archives of Florida, Florida Memory.

Page 201: Drawing of Seminole chief, Coacoochee (Wild Cat). 18—. Black & white photoprint, 10 × 8 in. State Archives of Florida, Florida Memory.

Page 204: Painted portrait of Florida's 29th Governor Millard F. Caldwell. Between 1945 and 1949. Black & white photoprint, 10 × 8 in. State Archives of Florida, Florida Memory.

Page 206: President Truman receives shirt and bag from Seminole Indians—Everglades City, Florida. 1947. Black & white photoprint, 4 × 5 in. State Archives of Florida, Florida Memory.

Page 209: Sammons, Sandra Wallus. Seminole bingo sign. 1986. Color slide. State Archives of Florida, Florida Memory.

Page 210: Martin Tabert. 1921. Black & white photoprint, 10 × 8 in. State Archives of Florida, Florida Memory.

Page 212: Judge James Dean—Monroe County, Florida. 18—?. Black & white photonegative, 5 × 4 in. State Archives of Florida, Florida Memory.

Page 215: Bombing of home of NAACP member—Mims, Florida. 1951. Black & white photograph, 8 × 10 in. State Archives of Florida, Florida Memory.

Page 216: Micanopy, a Seminole chief. 1836. Color transparency, 9 × 7 in. State Archives of Florida, Florida Memory.

Page 217: Portrait of Congressman Josiah Thomas Walls. Between 1871 and 1876. Black & white photoprint, 10 × 8 in. State Archives of Florida, Florida Memory.

Andrew K. Frank is the Allen Morris Professor of History at Florida State University. He is the author of *Before the Pioneers: Indians, Settlers, Slaves, and the Founding of Miami* as well as numerous other books and articles on the history of Florida and the southeastern Indians. He received his PhD from the University of Florida.

J. Hendry Miller is collections manager at the Georgia Archives. He previously worked as a reference archivist for the State Archives of Florida, as a history instructor, and as an independent researcher. Miller is an expert in the history of Native Americans, the early Republic, and the American South. He received his PhD from Florida State University.

Tarah Luke is a reformatting and digital processing archivist at the Georgia Archives. Luke previously worked as an adjunct instructor at Florida State University, where she taught courses in early and modern American and European history. She received her PhD from Florida State University.